Far Above Rubies

Today's Virtuous Woman

Edited by
Herman Hanko

Reformed Free
Publishing Association

© 1992 Reformed Free Publishing Association
All rights reserved
Printed in the United States of America

Second printing 2001

No part of this book may be used or reprinted in any form without written permission from the publisher, except in the case of brief quotations used in a critical article or review

Reformed Free Publishing Association
4949 Ivanrest Ave.
Grandville MI 49418-9709
Phone: (616) 224-1518
Fax: (616) 224-1517
Website: www.rfpa.org
E-mail: mail@rfpa.org

ISBN 0-916206-42-4
LC Number 92-80354

Preface

The Bible is interested in women; which means that God Himself is interested in and concerned about women. Anyone who claims that the Bible is male-oriented and ignores women simply does not know the Scriptures.

Scripture is the infallibly inspired record of God's great covenantal work in Christ. In the Old Testament Scriptures, the work of God's covenant was the preservation of the seed of the covenant so that Christ could be born in the fullness of time. Women are repeatedly described as being the ones who, more than the men, were concerned with the preservation of the seed of the covenant and the coming of Christ.

A few examples will demonstrate the point

Sarah lived with the great burden of a barren womb and was, in her desire to bring forth the seed of the covenant, willing to give her maid as a concubine to her husband. But she herself became that mother by a miracle and in her joy shouted, "The Lord hath made me to laugh." Tamar, in her longing to have a part in bringing forth the Christ, went so far as to play the role of a prostitute to lure her father-in-law into fulfilling his covenant obligations. Even Judah himself had to admit that she was more righteous than he. We must not approve of such conduct, but the intensity of the longing of these women stands out as a remarkable demonstration of their covenant consciousness. Both were rewarded with a place in the line that brought Christ into our flesh.

Hannah showed more concern for the seed of the covenant than her spiritually dull husband; and, when the Lord heard her prayer, she was inspired to sing a song which in astonishingly remarkable ways resembled the song which Mary sang when she knew that she was to be the mother of the Lord. The Shunammite woman could agonize over the sickness of a son miraculously given her when her calloused husband had no idea of what her agony was all about. Jehoshabeath risked her life to preserve the seed royal when she hid Josiah because she knew that Athaliah's murderous intents were a direct attack against the promised line of Christ.

How often was it not true that when the state of the true religion burned feebly in Israel and Judah, godly women manifested greater concern for the promises and covenant of God than the men. Scripture reminds us that these patterns are often true throughout the ages of the church. Indeed, already in Scripture there were times when the spiritual decline of the nation was so great that no man could be found to occupy important and crucial positions in the nation; and God shamed the nation and its men with a Deborah or a Hulda.

The New Testament was no different. Mary is blessed among all women, for she was the mother of the Lord. Jesus was pleased to be served in His earthly needs by loving women, and those who gave their lives to care for the Lord were rewarded with being the first audience when angels preached the gospel of the resurrection.

Nor were the apostles neglectful of the importance of women in the life of the church. Phebe was commended to the church of Rome for her service to the church of Cenchrea. Priscilla was worthy of special mention on the pages of Scripture for her selfless service in the cause of the church. The list of such women is long and filled with noble and godly saints without whose work the church would have been immeasurably impoverished. One thinks only of Lydia, of Lois and Eunice, of Dorcas, and many others. And how significant it is that Paul himself earnestly instructed Timothy not to neglect the important role which older women and widows must assume within the life of the church where Timothy was pastor.

Towering above all these passages is the eloquent and moving doxology of praise to the virtuous woman which the Holy Spirit sang through the wise man of Israel recorded for us in Proverbs 31.

It is important and striking that Scripture's high regard for women is always very carefully associated with the role which women occupy in God's kingdom and covenant by virtue of their creation and relation to man. The Scriptures say as it were: "God has given women a glorious place by virtue of their very creation. Move them out of their God-given place and load them with work and responsibilities which are not theirs by divine assignment or by nature and you create a monstrosity, of no use to God or the church. Acknowledge and cherish their role assigned by the Creator of all and Redeemer of the church and their work is of such incomparable value and blessing to the cause of God that only heaven will reveal the extent of it all."

In our day the feminist movement has taken control of life and has cast long and ugly shadows over the church. It is the determined intent of feminism, in all its rebellion against God's Word and the creation ordinance, to move women out of the place given them of God and put them in places where God has forbidden them to walk and work. Such rebellion not only mocks God's Word and law, but also deprives women of their glory and blessedness, forcing upon them roles which they are unable to fill, and which are denied them by virtue of greater callings given them by an all-wise Creator. Such insults to women bring shame and degradation upon the church and rob the church of the great profit she has always received from those women who served their Lord faithfully in the place ordained for them.

The faithful, men and women alike, raise their voices in protest and anger against this folly. Such feminism is not, the faithful insist, a deliverance of women from the slavery of male domination; it is an ugly imposition upon women of that which is unseemly and which destroys their beauty. The true church will not permit herself to be robbed of such a great blessing as that which comes from women who mean so much to the welfare of God's kingdom and covenant.

It is this protest which is raised in the book now sent out to the church and world in which we live. The publishers have gathered pamphlets, speeches, sermons, and articles from various sources and brought them together into a book which is much needed in our day. It is not a book which is negative: a vendetta against those who corrupt the Scriptures and rob women of their glory — although the evils of our age are carefully pointed out. It is a book which shows the great glory of covenant women. It is a book to encourage such covenant women in their calling, for the church knows that without the faithful labors of these mothers in Israel, the church is the loser.

May God bless these labors to the glory of His great name.

Herman C. Hanko
February 5, 1992

Table of Contents

A Virtuous Woman
    by Steven R. Key 3
The Key to a Happy Marriage
    by James Slopsema 19
The Christian Woman as Wife
    by David J. Engelsma 33
The Hope of the Covenant Mother in the Old Dispensation
    by Cornelius Hanko 47
Children in Marriage
    by David J. Engelsma 59
The Calling of the Truly Liberated Woman
    by Kenneth Koole 71
Letter to Timothy
    by Herman C. Hanko 87
When Thou Sittest in Thine House, by Abraham Kuyper
    She Girdeth Her Loins With Strength 105
    The Ways of Her House 110
    A Virtuous Woman 115
    Can a Woman Forget Her Sucking Child? 120
Phebe: An Example for the Christian Woman
    by Herman C. Hanko 127
Women in Church Office
    by Robert D. Decker 141
The Calling of Women in Church Office
    by Ronald Cammenga 157
Women Serving God
    by Steven R. Key 175

A Virtuous Woman

Steven R. Key

No single passage in all Scripture extols the virtues of a covenant wife and mother with greater eloquence than Proverbs 31:10-31. In this chapter, Rev. Steven Key, pastor of the Randolph Protestant Reformed Church of Randolph, Wisconsin, examines this passage in detail and points out the excellencies of a virtuous woman whose value is greater than rubies.

A Virtuous Woman

An Exposition of Proverbs 31:10-31

Who can find a virtuous woman? for her price is far above rubies.
The heart of her husband doth safely trust in her, so that he shall have no need of spoil.
She will do him good and not evil all the days of her life.
She seeketh wool, and flax, and worketh willingly with her hands.
She is like the merchants' ships; she bringeth her food from afar.
She riseth also while it is yet night, and giveth meat to her household, and a portion to her maidens.
She considereth a field, and buyeth it: with the fruit of her hands she planteth a vineyard.
She girdeth her loins with strength, and strengtheneth her arms.
She perceiveth that her merchandise is good: her candle goeth not out by night.
She layeth her hands to the spindle, and her hands hold the distaff.
She stretcheth out her hand to the poor; yea, she reacheth forth her hands to the needy.
She is not afraid of the snow for her household: for all her household are clothed with scarlet.
She maketh herself coverings of tapestry; her clothing is silk and purple.
Her husband is known in the gates, when he sitteth among the elders of the land.
She maketh fine linen, and selleth it; and delivereth girdles unto the merchant.
Strength and honour are her clothing; and she shall rejoice in time to come.
She openeth her mouth with wisdom; and in her tongue is the law of kindness.
She looketh well to the ways of her household, and eateth not the bread of idleness.
Her children arise up, and call her blessed; her husband also, and he praiseth her.
Many daughters have done virtuously, but thou excellest them all.
Favour is deceitful, and beauty is vain: but a woman that feareth the Lord, she shall be praised.
Give her of the fruit of her hands; and let her own works praise her in the gates.

Proverbs 31:10-31 sets before us the portrait of a beautiful woman in Israel. The passage says nothing about her physique, about her facial features or her figure. But it sets before us a most beautiful woman, a woman with a striking beauty that is seen only in Israel, the church of God. The wise mother of Lemuel had warned her royal son against the seduction of evil women and connected temptations, and had given him the fundamental rules for governing his kingdom. She now sets before him this full-length portrait of a virtuous woman, that choicest gift, which is said emphatically in Proverbs 19:14 to be from Jehovah.

You must understand, this portrait is that of a particular and special woman. This description of a virtuous woman would have been impossible with reference to a woman in the countries of the East outside Israel. There the woman was regarded only as a plaything and a slave. A virtuous woman, as described here, is definitely not some kind of underclass person. This portrait is also far removed from that of the modern woman. This woman is neither a doll figure nor one in the public limelight; certainly not the woman whose portrait would sell thousands of magazines each month in our country. Her kingdom is the home. Her works praise her in the gates. But it is her husband, and not she, that sits there among the elders.

The necessity of this portrait is clear from our own experience and is expressed in the text itself. This is recorded for the church of Christ as a portrait to be held in esteem by her. And in this day when the woman's features and virtues are being redrawn along entirely different lines, we must return to the Word of God and to this portrait of elegance and beauty. Every woman who confesses the name of Christ is called by God to pattern herself after this portrait of a virtuous woman.

Furthermore, the emphasis upon the importance of this portrait is seen in the original Hebrew by the form of the text. We have here an acrostic, i.e., each verse begins with the next letter of the Hebrew alphabet. The first verse, verse 10, begins with the Hebrew *aleph*, what we would call the letter "a." The next verse with what we would call the letter "b." Each verse begins with one of the 22 letters of the Hebrew alphabet in order. The purpose for such an order was to make it easier for this passage to be memorized by God's people.

So important is this passage for the lives of God's people, that it should be memorized. These verses should be memorized by girls and young women, that they may model their lives after this portrait. It should be memorized by boys and young men, that they may have always before them *this* portrait of true beauty and that, should they marry, their desire may be for such a godly woman. This passage ought to be memorized even by parents, that they may be training their daughters and the young women of the church to be the kind of women set forth here. This passage ought to be placed upon the hearts even of the elderly women, that they might, in accordance with Titus 2, teach the younger women. In fact, this ought to be in the minds of us all, that we might know how our sisters in the Lord reflect the glorious beauty of Christ's bride, the church.

This woman is a woman of many virtues, but the root of them all is found in the conclusion of verse 30. She is "a woman that feareth Jehovah."

The Bible always insists that the true beauty of women is spiritual.

God created woman a special being, fit perfectly for the man. Eve possessed a physical beauty that initially was not marred in any sense. She did not bear the curse in her body in the beginning. And therefore, she was an object of perfect beauty *physically*. Nor was that taken away from women. The Scripture recognizes the physical beauty and charm of the woman. The Song of Solomon is replete with that recognition of the woman's beauty, as Solomon reflects the love of Christ for His bride, the church. A woman ought not think that it is part of godliness that she pay no attention to her physical appearance. It is far from being a virtue, that a woman is a slob, either in her housekeeping or in her appearance. This virtuous woman pictured in Proverbs 31 is a woman who lives to reflect the glory of God's Being in her very appearance, also for the sake of her husband. That is implied in verse 22, where we read, "She maketh herself coverings of tapestry; her clothing is silk and purple." She dresses according to her station in life and certainly is not slovenly in appearance.

It is fitting in this connection to make a few more comments. It is possible that with some this aspect of the appearance of the virtuous woman will be more pleasing than any other aspect of her beauty. After all, this allows for some expenditures and some fine clothing and the like. Others may well be uncomfortable with this allowance, especially in the light of other passages of Scripture, where Isaiah and Zephaniah, Paul and Peter, testify *against* that vanity of dress and jewelry which is coveted by some women. Let us understand, therefore, the Bible does not condemn the use of jewelry as such, nor the wearing of fine clothing, but condemns *excess* which draws attention and covers up the beauty of holiness. And Lemuel's mother taught her son nothing contrary to that truth.

Notice, when the text mentions the clothing of the virtuous woman, it purposefully follows that which goes before. If the virtuous woman is clothed with silk and purple, it is because she has earned it by her good management and stewardship. Moreover, she cares for those who have need *before* looking to herself. She does not spend on a dress that which might support a needy family in the church. And even though she can afford such finery, she does not look upon herself as too superior to perform such other duties as are mentioned in this text. From all this we learn that the inspired writer allows costly apparel to the woman who can afford it, after the performance of those duties owed to her family and to the poor.

But the emphasis in this description of the virtuous woman is that she is *holy*. A virtuous woman is a woman who is an object of God's grace, an object which has received a make-over in God's spiritual beauty parlor. Her beauty is a spiritual beauty that will never fade away. That is why her physical beauty is hardly seen in comparison to the magnificent beauty which is this woman's spiritual beauty.

In fact, the Bible so emphasizes the spiritual beauty of the woman, that Solomon tells us graphically in Proverbs 11:22, that without that spiritual beauty, an attractive woman is like a pig with a jewel in its snout. An attractive personality is deceitful and physical beauty is vain. Of that you may be sure. "But a woman that feareth the Lord, she shall be praised." A virtuous woman is one who knows God. She loves God with such a love that she is afraid to offend Him in any way. She stands in awe of Him and lives her whole life as a woman before His face, striving to live out of love and reverence to Him. To put it in the language of the apostle Peter in I Peter 3, her beauty is not the mere outward beauty of the braiding of hair or being clothed in the latest fashions, nor in the application of paint and jewelry. But her adorning is that of the hidden man of the heart, that of a meek and quiet spirit, well pleasing unto God. This is the spiritual make-over, we might say, that is done only by God.

And therefore a virtuous woman is a woman gifted with wisdom.

A Virtuous Woman

The fear of the Lord, after all, is the beginning of wisdom, you read in Proverbs 9:10, as well as in other passages. And the point is, the virtuous woman is the woman who is in *Christ*, and who has Christ as her own. No wonder, then, that the price of a virtuous woman is far above rubies. God made her such a woman at the cost of His own Son's life. Christ is wisdom personified, as we see in Proverbs 8. Yes, to everyone but the fool, wisdom is far more precious than earthly jewels. And that is why, too, the price of a virtuous woman is beyond that of rubies. She is a gift of God to her husband. And it is God's work in her through Jesus Christ that sanctifies every part of her and makes her shine forth to His glory in all that she does.

But this means, furthermore, that the thing we should long to see in a woman is the fear of Jehovah. That is what young women should look for in themselves. The fear of Jehovah is what young men must require in the young women that they marry, and therefore in any women that they date. That is what parents must look for in their daughters, and what all the people of God must encourage in their sisters. For that fear of Jehovah in a woman we must rejoice when we see it. The fear of Jehovah is the root of virtue in the woman portrayed in Proverbs 31.

With the root of her virtue being the fear of Jehovah, is it a wonder that the question immediately asked is this: Who can find a virtuous woman?

When we examine that question, then we might say that one of the reasons a virtuous woman is so difficult to find is because rarely is she sought. Of course, the question "Who can find a virtuous woman?" is addressed to a young man. And yet we ask: Who among the young men are seeking for a virtuous woman?

Certainly the men in the world are not seeking for such a woman. This is not the woman whose face graces the covers of the world's magazines. This is not a woman whose picture you find in the magazine ads for cars and swimsuits and beer and liquor. A *virtuous* woman is a woman who is going to make a man of the world feel very out of place by her godliness.

But it is evident that there are many young men in the *church* who are seeking a woman other than a virtuous woman. Young men even in the church often look only for a woman with physical attractiveness and charm. And if a girl lacks what the advertisers are looking for in a "cover girl," even if she is marked by godliness and the fear of the Lord, then many young men in the church look away from her. Who is looking for a virtuous woman? I warn you, if you look for less, then the Lord may well give you what you are looking for; and you can spend a life-time learning that "favor is deceitful and beauty is vain." How many men are there, even in the church, whose lives are a little bit like hell, because God gave them that pretty she-devil that they were seeking? And Solomon, who himself fell from following after the wisdom of Jehovah, spoke from his own bitter experience, when he wrote in Proverbs 25:24: "It is better to dwell in the corner of the housetop, than with a brawling woman and in a wide house." And again in Proverbs 27:15: "A continual dropping in a very rainy day and a contentious woman are alike."

But then I ask the women, and particularly the young women, is this virtuous woman the type of woman you strive to be and to become? Who can find a virtuous woman? That is a valid question even in the sphere of the church, just as it was a valid question in Israel when this proverb was written. A young woman ought to ask herself in the light of this passage: Am I looking to cultivate the fear of the Lord as my most important quality, without exception? Are my most important exercises those spiritual exercises unto godliness — those exercises of devotion, of prayer, of training myself in the ways of a virtuous woman? Or are my most important exercises the *physical* exercises that seek to improve my attractiveness to young men, and is my bible the wretched and ungodly magazines published for the teenagers and women of this wicked world?

Who can find a virtuous woman? Are we parents teaching our daughters the ways of a virtuous woman? Or when we talk to and about our daughters is our conversation focused on their physical achievements and talents and popularity and potential career choices and so on? How many parents are there, in the church, who taught their daughters much of the world's ways, but little of God's ways? And how many parents are there who weep bitterly when they see the spiritual emptiness and devastating consequences of sin and misery in the daughters they raised? A virtuous woman is a rarity. Blessed are they who strive to bring up their daughters in the fear of the Lord. And blessed are those women whom God has established as virtuous women.

The fear of the Lord, which is the root of a godly woman's virtue, comes to expression.

The fear of the Lord cannot help but affect her behavior, as is set forth in many of the verses in this passage, first with respect to her place as a wife. The virtuous woman of Proverbs 31 is a married woman. That is certainly not to say that an unmarried woman cannot be a virtuous woman. But as a general rule it is the will of *God* that women marry. There are many exceptions, of course, by the providential government and good will of God. And they who are single show themselves virtuous women in a way somewhat different from the way set forth in this text, although the principle of the fear of God remains. But ordinarily it is the will of God that a woman express her fear of God in the sphere of marriage, marriage which, as all Scripture teaches, is to be established with one God-fearing man and until death brings separation. We note, however, that this is quite a different picture from that of the woman in the world today. A virtuous woman does not forsake marriage in order to pursue a career. A virtuous woman who is married does not live a glamorous life in the sphere of the work place, seeking the fulfillment and the rewards that the women of this world seek, and giving her marriage and family second place to her career. That is not the pattern set forth in this text. Quite the contrary. Again, the kingdom of this wife in Israel is the home.

The woman who fears Jehovah expresses her virtue in marriage, first of all, by faithfulness to her husband in all things. That truth is expressed in verses 11 and 12: "The heart of her husband doth safely trust in her, so that he shall have no need of spoil. She will do him good and not evil all the days of her life." When a man has a virtuous woman for his wife, he has a marriage where there is trust. Her faithfulness, her oneness of heart for God and therefore for him, her husband, leaves his heart at peace.

Parenthetically, it is worth noting that the same faithfulness should characterize her husband. You are aware of the fact that there was polygamy in the Old Testament. Men were unfaithful to their one wife, and took several. But whenever the Bible speaks of the God-ordained state, it speaks of marriage as one man with one woman. The blessing of Jehovah rests upon a marriage where there is mutual trust because of the love of God on the part of both. When a man is blessed with a virtuous woman, then he commits many things to her care and he leaves her each day to perform her labors *knowing* that his own interests are safe with her. The husband of this virtuous woman need not look with suspicion into the matters he has entrusted to her. He has no reservations or jealousies. Ruling in his own sphere outside of the home, he encourages her to rule well in her sphere within. And she conducts her business in the home so well that her husband has no need of spoil, i.e., no temptation to go after unjust gain, to enrich himself with the soldiers' spoils. A faithful wife and a confiding husband thus mutually bless each other.

Furthermore, this virtuous woman expresses her virtue by her submission to her husband. Her husband's comfort is her interest, and to live for him to the glory of God is her greatest happiness. "She will do him good and not evil all the days of her life." That is an expression of total submission. Let the ungodly stumble over that truth, but don't you. All that follows in this passage — her seeking of wool and flax, her willing handiwork, her rising early, her buying of a field, her sewing and so on — *all* that follows is just a detailed account of what is stated in verse 12, "She will do him good and not evil all the days of her life."

That this is something that causes women to rise up in rebellion today ought not surprise us. Again, "Who can find a virtuous woman? for her price is far above rubies." A virtuous woman is one who fears the *Lord*. And, therefore, she is one who does not obey the will of the flesh and the teaching of the National Organization for Woman — which is no more *for* women than the devil is *for* Christ. A virtuous woman obeys the will of God and walks according to the Word of God. And she knows that the will of God is laid down for her from the beginning, when God made Eve a *help* fit for Adam. That place as a submissive helper is not a cursed position. That was given the perfectly created woman *before* the fall. A virtuous woman sees herself as a *help* for her husband, nothing more and nothing less.

In the second place, this fear of the Lord which is the root of her virtue comes to expression in her labors as a homemaker.

Although it is true that this beautiful portrait of a virtuous woman is drawn in the setting of ancient Israel, the general principles set forth here are of universal application. There are as many elements to this idea as there are verses from 13-27. But all are summarized by that first statement of verse 27: "She looketh well to the ways of her household." We might well put it this way, as we find in Proverbs 14:1, a godly woman *builds* her house. So important is the God-fearing woman to her house and the house of her husband, that without her — as a virtuous woman in Christ — that house is not *built*.

Let us look at some of the principles set forth in the minute details of this portrait. We notice as a prominent factor that this virtuous woman is energetic in her labors. And although I realize there are limits to every woman's energy supply, and especially the energy supply of a mother, the principle here is that of self-denial.

Now, this woman had servants. Most women of the church today would like to point to that as the reason that the woman pictured in Proverbs 31 had such energy for her labors. After all, most women today do not have household servants, do they? It is true, except perhaps for the little help their children provide, or maybe much help on the part of some of their older children, women today do not have servants like this woman had. But women today have mechanical servants that the woman of King Lemuel's time never dreamed about! They did not have washing machines and dryers, microwave ovens, or even stoves and refrigerators! They did not even have running water! They did not have mechanical sewing machines and computers to track their investments. How many servants do we have today, compared to those women of the Old Testament? If anything, women today have an advantage in the number of servants!

But, notice, the virtuous woman is fully occupied with what many would consider the most mundane tasks. She goes before her servants as an example in diligence, rising before them to lay out the decree (the "portion" of verse 15), telling them what to do during that day. She imposes nothing upon them which she herself has not done before. She rules her household by efficient government. She seeks out material; her needle is at the service of her family. Instead of murmuring at what needs to be done, she sets the pattern of working willingly with her hands. By her own labors and by the wise management of money she does not hesitate to contribute to the happiness of her family, even by bringing in food from afar. She cooks for her family. Instead of lounging around or sitting with her ear and mouth to the telephone, she counts it no shame to be working at the sewing machine, i.e., at the spindle and distaff. Her whole soul is committed to building her household and doing her husband good, girding her loins with strength, and strengthening her arms.

Now, there are a couple elements of this passage that we ought to consider more closely in this connection.

There are those in our day who would appeal to Proverbs 31 to prove that a godly wife can have at the same time a family and a career outside of the household. They have found that especially in verses 16 and 24. And therefore we ought to consider those verses a moment. In verse 16, there are those who would like to point out that this virtuous woman was a real estate agent. That, however, is not the case. When you read in verse 16, "She considereth a field, and buyeth it," that does not mean that she is in the real estate business. Rather, she is adding a field to the estate, to the farm of the householder, for the good of her husband. That is evident when you read further, "with the fruit of her hands she planteth a vineyard." And notice, for the good of her husband she *considereth* this field. She does not go and buy something on a whim, but she judges whether it is worth the money. And what she buys she seeks to make fruitful, planting a vineyard for the supply of her household. And when she maketh fine linen and selleth it, the idea is not that she has a retail clothing business. But she works in the home, providing her household with a little extra income by delivering to the merchants the clothing that she makes. But notice also the *place* of this particular text. (The Holy Spirit places these verses in a particular order.) She makes this fine linen, these girdles, only after taking care of all her other labors. Only after providing her family with good meals and winter clothing, etc., does she turn to her projects for the merchants.

There is nothing in this passage to suggest that she divides her interests between household and career. And this is not because she *needs* to cook, and she *needs* to sew. She is not stuck in the home because she cannot afford daycare for her children. She does this work because she *ought* to do it and because she *wants* to do it, for the fear of the Lord and for the sake of her husband. If, as we read in Psalm 104:23, "Man goeth forth unto his work and to his labor until the evening," then we also must submit willingly to the Word of God when we are told in Titus 2:5 that the wife and mother finds her work as a "keeper at home." That limits the expression of her gifts not a bit. That does not confine her in the four walls of her house. Quite the contrary. She is one busy woman, a wise woman, a woman who does what needs to be done for the benefit of her household and the household of God.

And finally, concerning the expression of her virtue, we certainly may not overlook those expressions of her fear of the Lord which are specifically expressions of her spirituality. A virtuous woman, as set before us in this text, seeks not only the welfare of her immediate family, but she also seeks the welfare of the family of God. That you read in verse 20: "She stretcheth out her hand to the poor; yea, she reacheth forth her hands to the needy."

Some women have nothing for those in need, and even begrudge the fact that their husbands take some of what they perceive as their own and give it to the poor, or to the church for the work of the ministry. There are other women who appear from many perspectives to be like this portrait. But there is a major shortcoming. They coop themselves up in their own little world, paying attention only to their own household, and showing no concern for the family of God. We must realize that our own little households are only a small part of the kingdom of God, and that they are nothing without the other parts of the body of Christ. A virtuous woman loves her household as it belongs to the kingdom of God and of Christ. And, therefore, she loves all who belong to that kingdom. And she shows this by extending her hand to the poor, and providing for those in need.

A jewel in her godliness is this virtuous woman. That is also seen in verse 26, where we read: "She openeth her mouth with wisdom; and in her tongue is the law of kindness." That her mouth expresses wisdom shows that she does not neglect the means whereby God *bestows* that wisdom, namely, the preaching of the Word and the devotional life of the believer. Many women neglect the spiritual side, and as a result speak much foolishness. A virtuous woman may not speak much, but her speech is a joy, for it is characterized by wisdom. And that wisdom is the wisdom of God, the wisdom of His Word. She speaks that wisdom to her children, teaching them even as she is feeding and clothing them.

Then also, "in her tongue is the law of kindness." She is not a harsh woman, one to drive people away with her contentious words. She is not one to tear the church apart with her wretched gossip and slander. When she speaks, she speaks with kindness, expressing the fear of Jehovah.

Blessed is the fruit given to such a woman.

In the first place, "her husband is known in the gates, when he sitteth among the elders of the land."

A virtuous woman receives that as her blessedness. To understand that, we must understand her husband's place. You must not have the idea from verse 23 that the husband of this virtuous woman is an unemployed, lazy, good-for-nothing, who sits by the gate of the city while his wife works her fingers to the bone. The gate of the city was the place where the elders of Israel gathered. There they were busy with the rule of the nation; there they were judging the matters of the church. The woman was not there. She did not want to be, nor was she allowed by God to be. The same holds true today. In I Timothy 2:11, 12, we read, "Let the women learn in silence with all subjection. But I suffer not a woman to teach, nor to usurp authority over the man, but to be in silence." That Word of God is enough for a virtuous woman. Her place is not in the gates, ruling in Israel. And if a woman is found today holding an office in the church of Jesus Christ, she may have all kinds of gifts, but she lacks the one fundamental gift which is required of an officebearer. She is void of the fear of the Lord. For the fear of the Lord expresses itself in obedience to the Word of God.

Yet, we ought also to see that this man sits in the gate and is honored largely because of the wife that God has given him. That is why also this belongs to the fruit of a virtuous woman. We see that clearly in I Timothy 3, where one of the qualifications for an officebearer is the *wife* that he has, and that his children are in subjection. Although the husband bears the responsibility for the wife and what goes on with his children, nevertheless, the point is clear: the actual performance in one's household depends in large part upon the woman there, and whether or not she is a virtuous woman. This man sits in the gate. And the honor of her husband is pleasing to his wife. The blessed fruit of her virtue is seen in her husband. Thereby do her own works praise her in the gates. And let all who fear God honor her.

Furthermore, a virtuous woman finds herself blessed in the affection and praise given her by her family.

Oftentimes because of sin children fail to recognize the blessedness of their virtuous mother. For one thing, we are not perfect on this earth. The woman who makes up the portrait of this text is not a perfect woman, either. She fails often. She is described here, not according to the way she always conducted herself, but according to the power and principle that controlled her life. For her shortcomings and sins there was forgiveness in the blood of Christ. God-fearing women today experience this also. Children must see that, too. Children do not see so clearly the blessedness of their virtuous mother. But without fail, as they grow up in the Lord and take their place in the church, and especially as they find themselves surrounded with children of their own, they find their mother constantly before consciousness. Her tender guidance, her wise instruction, her loving discipline, her holy example, form a portrait that they in turn strive to imitate. They look upon that virtuous woman and cease not to call her blessed and to thank God for her whose price is far above rubies.

No less warmly does her husband praise her. As the years fade that beauty of youth, the bond between husband and wife only becomes stronger, because of the fear of Jehovah. That man is rich to whom God has given a virtuous woman. Such a man cannot count his riches, they are so great! For the price of a virtuous woman is far above rubies. Thank God for her! Thank God for all the virtuous women in His church! Without them there would be no church. And let us instruct our daughters and sons, that the sons of the church may continue to find virtuous women, until the church is gathered and God Himself praises those virtuous monuments to His glory.

The Key to a Happy Marriage

James Slopsema

Love is the cement which binds husband and wife together in a happy marriage. This love is first of all God's love for His elect people in Christ. The love which must be present in marriage is the fruit and reflection of God's love for us. Rev. James Slopsema delivered this speech at a family conference sponsored by the Evangelism Committee of the South Holland, Illinois, Protestant Reformed Church. Rev. Slopsema is pastor of the Hope Protestant Reformed Church in Walker, Michigan.

The Key to a Happy Marriage

For many marriage has been a bitter disappointment. Expecting to find bliss, they have found marriage to be a frequent source of frustration, anger, bickering, and sometimes even fear. Irreconcilable differences, alcoholism, wife-abuse, unfaithfulness are just a few of the problems that are common-place in marriage today. Small wonder that almost one out of every two marriages in our country is ending in divorce and that many other marriages are in deep trouble. Almost everyone has a close relative or friend who is either divorced or whose marriage is in trouble. Some reading these words may have a troubled marriage.

There are no easy answers when it comes to solving marital problems. This is certainly the experience of any couple which has seriously faced the problems in its own marriage and has tried to overcome them. Sometimes the problems in marriage seem to be insurmountable so that a couple will be tempted to look to divorce as the only solution.

Husbands and wives need to be assured that there are no problems in marriage that are insurmountable. With the Bible as our guide we must rest assured that with God all things are possible (cf. Matt. 19:26) and that we can do all things through Christ who strengthens us (Phil. 4:13). In God's power which reaches us in Jesus Christ we are even able to solve those "impossible" problems that arise in marriage. No one who belongs to Jesus Christ needs to despair in the face of marital problems. He will find the answers to all his problems in the Bible. And in Jesus Christ his Savior he will find the power to put the solutions of the Bible into practice so that he will have a happy marriage.

The Key Is Love

It ought to be obvious that the heart of marriage is love. It is love for one another that brings a man and woman into marriage, and it is love that sustains their marriage. If the love between husband and wife grows cold, their marriage loses its life and often ends in divorce. For that very reason God repeatedly calls husbands to love their wives (and by implication wives to love their husbands). In Ephesians 5:25 husbands are called to love their wives just as Christ loved the church and gave Himself for it. Here we find the key to a happy marriage. Husband and wife must love each other just as Christ loves His church. When there is that kind of love in a marriage, it will be a happy one. The root of every marital problem is to be found in a failure of husband and wife to love one another as Christ loves His church.

Much of the love we find in marriage today is a false, imitation love. We all know what an imitation is. An imitation is something that in many ways looks like the real thing but is not the real thing. It is only a fake, a fraud. In the same way the love that characterizes many marriages today is a fraudulent love. It is a love that in many ways resembles real love. But if put to the test of the Bible, it becomes quite apparent that this love is only a cheap imitation.

This imitation love that characterizes so much of marriage today is an attraction to one's spouse because of what one's spouse can do for him or her. This imitation love is rooted in a basic concern for self. Those who have this imitation love in marriage are basically concerned about themselves. They are concerned with their own needs, their own desires, their own pleasure, their own happiness. They are really not concerned with others; they are concerned with themselves. But then they meet someone of the opposite sex whom they feel is not only able but also willing to meet their needs. This other person can supply their sexual needs. This person will help them achieve their goals in life, will protect them, will provide for them, and will make them happy. And so they are attracted to this person and in due time develop a relationship with this person which finally culminates in marriage. To the degree that this characterizes the love between a man and a woman whether before or in marriage, to that degree their love for each other is only an imitation.

Certainly this kind of love resembles a true, genuine love because it is a deep attraction for someone else and a desire to share one's life with another. However, it is fraudulent because it is basically a self-centered love, a love that is concerned chiefly about self. The Bible teaches us that genuine love is not selfish. In I Corinthians 13 we find a beautiful chapter devoted to charity or love. In verse 5 we read that love "seeketh not her own." In Luke 6:32, 33 Jesus taught, "For if ye love them which love you, what thank have ye? for sinners also love those that love them. And if ye do good to them that do good to you, what thank have ye? for sinners also do even the same." The point here is that there is nothing to a love that loves only when there is something to be had in return. This is a false love.

A true, genuine love is altogether different from this in that it is patterned after God's love for His people in Jesus Christ.

There are three elements to God's love for man.

First, God's love is not dependent on man's love for Him. Rather, God's love is always first. God loves man even though man hates Him. In fact, God's love creates love for Himself in man's heart. This is certainly what Paul implied in Romans 5:8, "But God commendeth his love toward us, in that, while we were yet sinners, Christ died for us." This is also the implication of I John 4:10, "Herein is love, not that we loved God, but that he loved us, and sent his son to be the propitiation for our sins." And then consider verse 19 of the same chapter, "We love him, because he first loved us."

Secondly, God in His love seeks the welfare of man. On account of his sin, man is hopelessly lost. Man is headed for hell, and there is nothing he can do to save himself. Yet God in His love saves man in Jesus Christ from certain destruction and brings him to a heavenly glory which he has neither earned nor deserves.

Finally, God in His love is willing to sacrifice for the welfare and salvation of man. For the salvation of man, God was willing even to sacrifice His own Son on the cross. "For God so loved the world, that he gave his only begotten Son, that whosoever believeth in him should not perish, but have everlasting life" (John 3:16).

True love among men, and this applies to the love between a man and woman in marriage, also has these same three elements.

This becomes apparent from what Jesus said in the great Sermon on the Mount, "Ye have heard that it hath been said, Thou shalt love thy neighbor, and hate thine enemy. But I say unto you, Love your enemies, bless them that curse you, do good to them that hate you, and pray for them which despitefully use you, and persecute you" (Matt. 5:43, 44).

Notice that Jesus instructs us to love even our enemies. Our enemies are described as those who hate us, curse us, despitefully use us, and persecute us. Without any stretch of the imagination we can say that this enemy is sometimes one's marriage partner. Marriage can get that bad. And our natural response is, "Do not expect me to love you when you do not care for me and mistreat me like that!" But Jesus says to love your spouse anyway. Do not make your love dependent on your spouse first loving you and doing good to you. Love your spouse regardless of whether he loves you. Love your spouse even if he is your enemy. Love your spouse first and by your love encourage him to love you in return. That is genuine love!

Secondly, Jesus indicated how one is to show this love to his spouse. Jesus indicated that one shows his love to others by blessing them that curse him, doing good to them that hate him, and praying for those who despitefully use him. This holds true in marriage as well. Husbands and wives truly love each other when they do good to one another, pray for one another and bless one another. In other words, they are not each primarily concerned about their own interests but with the welfare and good of their spouses.

Finally, according to the pattern of God's love for man, true love in a marriage makes husband and wife willing to sacrifice for the welfare of one another. One who truly loves his spouse in marriage is willing to sacrifice his desires, his pleasure, his interests, his time, his reputation, if need be even his life for the welfare of his spouse.

Now that we have come to understand the love that a husband and wife are to have for each other in marriage, let us see what a difference this kind of love makes in marriage!

Overcoming Differences in Love

With this genuine love husbands and wives will be able to overcome what otherwise may be irreconcilable differences.

No two people are the same. A man and woman entering into marriage come from different homes and backgrounds. He comes from a home that does things one way; she comes from a home that does things a different way. It does not take long for a husband to realize that his wife does not cook like his mother does or for the wife to realize that her husband does not think much of some things that were so important in her own home and are still important to her. In addition to this, husband and wife soon find in marriage that both have their own opinions, interests, pet peeves, and goals which often conflict with that of their spouse.

And so for marriage to work there must be flexibility and compromise. There must be give and take. Husbands and wives must learn to adjust to each other. In some cases the husband must be willing to surrender to his wife's wishes; or the wife must be willing to do things her husband's way. In other matters, where neither one can conform to the pattern of the other, it is necessary that they find a middle course with which both can live. Ideally, husband and wife should seek to find their own way that is better than what either knew before they entered into marriage.

For this to take place it is very important that husband and wife have a true, genuine love for each other.

Compromise and adjustment in marriage becomes virtually impossible when a marriage is controlled by an imitation love of selfishness. The husband who loves his wife exactly because she is able to satisfy his needs and desires is not too inclined to let his wife have her way or to compromise with her. Everything must be his way. And the wife who is basically concerned with her needs, desires, and ambitions in life is also going to insist on having her way. After all, her husband exists basically for her sake. Why should she give in to him? The result of all this is that the differences between husband and wife become irreconcilable. Neither will give in to the other. There is constant fighting and hurting one another. The attraction for each other that once was so strong slowly disappears. They no longer love each other and may well file for divorce on the grounds of "irreconcilable differences." And the root of it all is that their love was only an imitation love.

What a difference a true, genuine love makes. If a marriage is controlled by a love that seeks the welfare of one another and is willing to sacrifice for one another, that marriage has the key to overcoming the differences that arise in it. Then neither partner will insist that everything must be his way. There will be a willingness to give in to the wishes and desires of the other. There will be an ability to compromise, to meet each other half-way. With a true love no problem or difference that arises in marriage is insurmountable.

Tolerating Weaknesses in Love

In a marriage controlled by genuine love, husband and wife will also be able to tolerate the weaknesses of one another.

Everyone has terrible weaknesses and faults. These weaknesses usually are not too apparent during courtship. During courtship each has a tendency to put his or her best foot forward. When weaknesses do surface, the assumption of many young couples is that they will change these undesirable traits in their beloved once they are married. What a myth that turns out to be! Young married couples find soon enough that its almost impossible to bring about drastic changes in one another. In fact, instead of disappearing, the weaknesses that each brings into marriage tend to limit and hurt the other.

In a marriage controlled by an imitation love of selfishness, these weaknesses tend to become unbearable.

For, first of all, one who loves his spouse because of what she can do for him will see no need to correct his faults or prevent his spouse from being hurt by them. Why should he change? Why should he try to correct his faults? Does not she exist for his sake? And so without any thought or concern for his spouse, he lets her bear the brunt of all his weaknesses. But woe to her if she allows her weaknesses and frailties to show! And woe to her if she, in her weakness, limits or hurts or embarrasses him in any way! That is intolerable! In fact, when marriage is controlled by selfish love, both husband and wife will be inclined to focus on and see only the weaknesses of one another. Each one being caught up in his own self-centered world will completely fail to see and appreciate the good points of the other. Rather each will focus on each other's weakness and find the weaknesses of the other unbearable. Such a marriage is in deep trouble.

What a difference a genuine love makes in this regard!

Those who in love are genuinely concerned with the welfare of their spouses will seek to recognize and control their weaknesses so that they do not repeatedly hurt their spouses through their weaknesses. They will find that they can not simply put away their faults. The weaknesses that characterize each of us are deeply ingrained so that in many cases we are never completely free of them. Everyone has certain weaknesses that he must fight all his life long. But those who genuinely love their spouses will seek to control their weaknesses to avoid hurting, if at all possible, their spouses.

In turn when love is genuine, husbands and wives will bear patiently with the weakness of each other. Being more concerned with the welfare of their spouses than with their own whim and desires, they will tend to bear patiently with the faults of their partners. Instead of tearing each other down, they will rather seek to help each other overcome their weaknesses. They will not focus their attention on the weaknesses of one another but will look beyond these weaknesses to see the strengths each has. This in turn fosters a deep appreciation for one another. Those who have this attitude toward each other in marriage have something going for them! They will have a happy marriage indeed!

Assuming in Love One's God-given Place in Marriage

In a marriage controlled by love both husband and wife will also assume their God-given places in marriage.

Contrary to popular opinion, marriage is not a democracy with husband and wife each having equal say. This arrangement would work if husband and wife always agreed. But as soon as there is disagreement democracy in marriage fails.

Marriage is an institution of God, ordained by God from the beginning of history. God created marriage when He brought Adam and Eve together as one flesh in the garden of Eden (Gen. 2). And God ordained that in marriage the husband is to be the head of the wife. That means that he is to rule his wife and to care for her. In turn, the wife is called by God to submit to the rule of her husband and to be a help to him. In Ephesians 5:22ff. we read, "Wives, submit yourselves unto your own husbands, as unto the Lord. For the husband is the head of the wife, even as Christ is the head of the church: and he is the savior of the body. Therefore, as the church is subject unto Christ, so let the wives be to their own husbands in everything."

When marriage is controlled by a false love of selfishness this arrangement tends to break down, often to the ruin of the marriage.

The husband who is selfish in his dealings with his wife tends to be a tyrant. He rules his wife with little if any consideration for her needs or wants. He rules his wife and family according to his own selfish whims.

In turn, the wife who is selfish in her dealings with her husband despises the rule of her husband. She will rebel against her husband's rule, either openly and vocally or perhaps underhandedly and sneakily. This rebellion may be occasioned by the tyranny of her husband.

But rebel she will. Nor will she be the help to her husband that God calls her to be. She will be a hinderance to him as she seeks to undermine his rule and have her own way in things.

The marriage in which this kind of thing is found is a troubled marriage full of fighting and bitterness.

How different when there is genuine love in a marriage where husband and wife are primarily concerned with the welfare of one another. In that marriage the husband is genuinely concerned with his wife's needs and desires as he rules her. In love he recognizes that woman is different from man with different needs and desires. Consequently, he takes the time and effort to acquaint himself with his wife's needs. (How few husbands ever do this.) And these needs of his wife he always takes into consideration. As the head of his wife and family he is the one who must make the decisions. His word is law in the home. But in ruling his wife he always has the welfare of his wife in mind. For that reason things do not always go his way. When it comes to matters of mere preference, more often than not the wishes of his wife will prevail.

In turn, the wife who truly loves her husband will desire to be the help God has called and equipped her to be. Realizing that there is nothing that will hinder her husband more than to undermine his rule, she willingly submits to his authority. Oh, she may disagree with him. And she may express her disagreement. She may even rebuke him if he persists in following a course contrary to the Bible. If he insists that she follow a sinful course of life, she must even disobey him. But even then she will not try to undermine him but will be submissive in spirit that she may truly be a help to him.

These are only a few of the differences genuine love for each other makes in a marriage.

Certainly there can be little doubt that the key to a happy, lasting marriage is a true, genuine love. Let husband and wife truly love one another and their marriage will be richly blessed.

How to Attain this Love in Marriage

To attain and maintain this kind of love in marriage it is necessary first to find a God-fearing partner in marriage.

This will become quite apparent if we bear in mind that only the born-again Christian is able to love in the genuine sense of the word. The ungodly unbeliever is not. The only love that the unbeliever is capable of is an imitation love. At the fall in the beginning of history mankind became horribly twisted and perverted spiritually. So twisted did he become that he is not even able to love in the true sense of the word. All he is capable of is a false, imitation love in which he is attracted to those whom he is convinced will serve his selfish purposes. To love in the true sense of the word as God loves man requires nothing less than a new birth in Jesus Christ. God must come into the heart and in His love work a radical change.

Hence, if we will have a truly happy marriage where there is true love, it is necessary that we find a godly partner for marriage. And this is the calling God places before all who enter into marriage. Speaking not just of marriage, but certainly of marriage also, the Bible tells us in II Corinthians 6:14, "Be not unequally yoked together with unbelievers." Speaking of those free to remarry after the death of their spouses, the Word of God warns that marriage is to be "only in the Lord" (I Cor. 7:39).

In a real sense, therefore, the key to a happy marriage begins long before marriage in seeking out a proper marriage partner. All too often young adults are overly concerned with superficial things in selecting a husband or wife. They want a person with good looks, a charming personality and a certain indefinable "sex appeal." However, these and other things that were so important before marriage soon enough lose their charm after a few years of marriage. Then what becomes all important is to have a partner who loves you unselfishly and who in love will stand with you to face life's harsh realities. Let every young man and woman seek that kind of marriage partner! Neither is this kind of partner difficult to recognize. He is the young man who is spiritually-minded. She is the young woman busily serving her God and others in love and not herself.

For many, however, this advice may be too late. Many have made the mistake of choosing marriage partners who had very little interest in spiritual matters. If they were born-again believers in Jesus Christ, they certainly did not show it in the way they lived. And now, quite consistent with their unspiritual approach to life, neither are they showing any true love in their marriages. They are completely self-centered, having all the sinful, undesirable characteristics that make for a disastrous marriage.

To those who find themselves with this kind of marriage partner the Bible has the following advice in I Peter 3:1: "Likewise, ye wives, be in subjection to your own husbands; that, if any obey not the word, they also may without the word be won by the conversation of the wives." This word of God is addressed to wives; it applies equally as well to husbands. What this word of God is saying is that those who have unbelieving spouses should work for the conversion of their spouses. They must win, if at all possible, their spouses to the Lord. And they are to do this by their own conversation or manner of living. They must in all their dealings with their spouses show a genuine love. The wives must refuse to become rebellious to their tyrannical husbands but instead be submissive. The husbands are to avoid becoming vindictive as they rule their wives but instead are to rule their wives in all love and kindness. God often will use this to bring conversion and faith to unbelieving spouses.

To attain genuine love in marriage however requires more than husband and wife being born-again believers capable of this love. It also requires that they grow in this love.

We must remember that even though genuine love beats in the heart of every born-again Christian, this love does not always show itself in his life. This is because every true Christian has a sinful nature. Sometimes the Bible calls this sinful nature of the Christian his flesh, sometimes the old man of sin. By whatever name it is called the sinful nature of the Christian is that aspect of his very being which has not yet been changed by the grace of God but is still under the power of sin. This sinful nature has a great deal of influence in the Christian's life. It constantly leads him astray into sin. And it constantly leads him to show an imitation love of selfishness toward others, especially it seems to the one closest to him, his spouse.

Every Christian couple knows this from many disappointing experiences of the past. Every Christian who has married in the Lord will certainly tell you that his spouse has not always dealt with him in genuine love and neither has he done so with his spouse. The experience of every Christian couple is that there is much false, imitation love in their marriage. And for that reason there are many problems in their marriage. In some cases the marriages of committed Christians are even in deep trouble.

Every Christian couple must learn to show to each other the true love Christ has put in their hearts for each other. They must grow in this love so that more and more they deal with one another in this love.

And this requires the grace of God in Jesus Christ. Nothing less than the irresistible grace of God is sufficient to overcome the power of the Christian's sinful nature with its destructive selfishness. In turn, nothing less than the irresistible grace of God is sufficient to strengthen the true love God has put in his heart that he may live in that love with his spouse.

This grace comes only by a faithful, diligent use of those means which God uses to work His grace in our hearts. The Christian couple receives the grace of God by faithfully attending church where the Word of God is faithfully preached and the sacraments (baptism and Lord's Supper) are properly administered. They receive the grace of God to love one another truly through their own faithful study of the Bible in their home and through their diligent prayers. And when in spiritual trouble, as many couples are, the grace of God reaches them through the help of their pastor, their elders, and their fellow saints.

Let every husband and wife fight the temptation to neglect these very important avenues through which God's grace reaches us. To the degree they do, they will be powerless to love one another truly. And their marriages will suffer.

Let every husband and wife make good use of every means of grace God has provided them in the church and their home, that in the riches of grace they may truly love one another and enjoy a rich, satisfying marriage.

The Christian Woman as Wife

David J. Engelsma

While pastor of the Loveland Protestant Reformed Church in Loveland, Colorado, Prof. David Engelsma delivered a series of sermons on marriage. These were later prepared for publication in a book entitled *Marriage: The Mystery of Christ and the Church.* This chapter is taken from the book and, on the basis of a careful exegesis of Titus 2:4, 5, explains the role of the wife in a covenantal marriage. Prof. Engelsma is now professor of Old Testament and Dogmatics in the Protestant Reformed Seminary in Grand Rapids, Michigan.

The Christian Woman as Wife

That they may teach the young women to be sober, to love their husbands, to love their children,
To be discreet, chaste, keepers at home, good, obedient to their own husbands, that the word of God be not blasphemed.
Titus 2:4, 5

According to this text, it is the duty of the older women in the church to instruct the younger women in their calling as wives. The text sets forth the calling of the young married women. But it is not the minister, Titus, who is to teach this to the young women directly. The minister must speak the things which become sound doctrine (2:1). He must speak to the older women (2:3), so that they in turn will teach the younger married women. The older women of the church, whether married or unmarried, have a definite responsibility to the younger women, a certain "office" to fulfill. There is good reason for this. The older women are able to do what the minister or the elder, as a man, is not as capable of doing. Naturally enough, the young women rely on the older women. They go to the older women with their questions and problems, so that the older women have the opportunity to instruct the young women. This is especially true of the older women who are mothers in Israel and who are, therefore, looked to by their daughters and daughters-in-law. They must make use of these opportunities to teach the young women to be sober, to love their husbands, to love their children, and to do all of the other duties of the text.

But the older women do not teach only by words. They are also called to teach by their example. The young wives see in the behavior of the older women a pattern that they should follow, especially in the behavior of their mothers. It is particularly the behavior of the older women toward their own husbands that is an influential example for the young women. The example that mothers give to their daughters is most effective instruction, whether for good or bad. From their earliest years, daughters should grow up in a home in which their mother's relationship to their father is the godly one set forth in Titus 2:4, 5. By means of their own life, the older women, and especially mothers, must be "teachers of good things."

Although the viewpoint is that of the calling of the older women to teach the younger, the text presents a complete description of the Christian young woman as wife. Our reaction to the young wife pictured here is, "What a beautiful and noble creature she is." She is glorious with the same glory that shines in the wife of Proverbs 31. She differs from the women of the world as beauty differs from ugliness and as nobility differs from baseness. Hers is genuine beauty and true adornment: "a meek and quiet spirit," as Peter says, "which is in the sight of God of great price" (I Pet. 3:4). "Her children arise up, and call her blessed; her husband also, and he praiseth her" (Prov. 31:28).

We find that her beauty and glory consist of three main virtues. She is obedient; she is sound-minded, or, as the text puts it, "sober" and "discreet"; she is God-fearing. This is the calling of every Christian woman as wife.

* * * * * * *

When one reads all of the passages in the New Testament that give the calling of a wife in marriage, he discovers that the fundamental calling is subjection to her husband. It is striking that the wife is only rarely told to love her husband. Over and over, the wife is called to be in subjection and to obey. This text in Titus is one of the few passages that mention the wife's love for her husband. The explanation for this is not, of course, the insignificance of the wife's love. Rather, the explanation is the tremendous importance of submission and obedience.

Consider several of the outstanding New Testament passages on the calling of the wife. Ephesians 5:22-33 admonishes: "Wives, submit yourselves unto your own husbands.... As the church is subject unto Christ, so let the wives be to their own husbands in every thing... [Let] the wife see that she reverence her husband." Colossians 3:18 exhorts: "Wives, submit yourselves unto your own husbands, as it is fit in the Lord." I Peter 3:1-6 contains the following instruction: "Ye wives, be in subjection to your own husbands; ... the holy women also, who trusted in God, adorned themselves, being in subjection unto their own husbands: Even as Sara obeyed Abraham, calling him lord." I Corinthians 11:3 says that "the head of the woman is the man." I Timothy 2:12 forbids the woman "to usurp authority over the man." There can be no question that God calls the wife to be in subjection to her husband and to obey, and that this is the basic calling of the wife. If this is present in her, the wife can also do the other things that are required of her. If this is lacking, she must fail in all the other aspects of her wifely calling also. If she is not in subjection, neither will she be sober, a lover of her husband and children, or good. For the wife, the virtue of subjection is crucial.

Paul mentions this virtue in Titus 2:5: "obedient to their own husbands." The word that is translated "obedient" in the text is the word that elsewhere in Scripture is translated "be in subjection," or "be submissive." The literal reading of verse 5 would be: "submissive to their own husbands." There is a distinction between "being submissive" and "obeying." First, they are two different words in the Bible. Both are found together in I Peter 3:5, 6: "The holy women also, who trusted in God, adorned themselves, *being in subjection* unto their own husbands: Even as Sara *obeyed* Abraham." The holy women in the Old Testament were in subjection, and they obeyed. Second, these two different words have their own distinct meaning. Being in subjection refers to the inner attitude of a wife's heart, according to which she knows her husband to be in authority over her and freely wills it. Subjection, or submission, is altogether invisible and secret. It is a matter of the heart, as is everything important. This is what Peter calls in I Peter 3:4 "the hidden man of the heart ... a meek and quiet spirit." Within, in her heart, the submissive wife consciously, actively places herself under the authority of the husband, as regards her person and her entire life. Obedience, in distinction from submission, refers to one's outward behavior. The obedient wife does what her husband tells her to do. But she does more than this. She lives her entire life in conformity with her husband's will.

Submission and obedience are related. Submission in the heart is the source and cause of obedience; obedience is the fruit and manifestation of submission. If a wife is in subjection to her husband, she will obey him. If a wife is disobedient to her husband, it is because she does not submit in her heart. The relationship is shown in I Peter 3:4, 5: Holy women of the past were in subjection to their husbands; therefore, like Sara, they obeyed their husbands. Submission is basic. Therefore, although it also requires obedience, Scripture stresses the calling of the wife to be in subjection. This is literally what we have in Titus 2:5: The young women must be in subjection to their husbands. This calling is absolute and unqualified. There are no exceptions. There are no circumstances that permit a wife to disregard this calling. Ephesians 5:24 is plain: "As the church is subject unto Christ, so let the wives be to their own husbands in every thing." When the Holy Spirit requires the wife to submit in everything, He not only refers to those things that belong to the mutual life of the husband and wife, for example, their own relationship, the running of the home, and the upbringing of the children, but He also includes everything that belongs to the wife's personal life.

Implied is the command that the wife be in subjection always. She must be in subjection when her husband lives with her according to knowledge, as he is required to do. But she must be in subjection also when he fails to do his calling and manifests himself as self-centered and harsh. Even when the wife cannot and may not obey, she can and must be in subjection. Nowhere does God require the woman to obey in everything. A husband might order his wife to sin, especially if the husband is an unbeliever. Even a believing husband might order an unreasonable, harmful, or evil action on the part of his wife. In such cases, the wife does not obey. But she still is in subjection. This will be evident in her demeanor as she disobeys. She does not disobey as a rebel, but meekly.

Wives can sin against the commandment of submission in two ways. A wife may be an out-and-out rebel against the lordship of her husband. She opposes and contradicts him. She disobeys and overrules him. The result is hellish confusion and warfare in the home, for the home now has two heads. There is no order, only chaos. If a woman persists in this rebellion, the warning of Romans 13:2 applies to her: "Whosoever therefore resisteth the power, resisteth the ordinance of God: and they that resist shall receive to themselves damnation." Another form of disobedience to the calling of the wife is the wife's ignoring of her husband and independently living her own life as she pleases. This is what the apostle refers to in I Timothy 2:12, when he speaks of the woman's usurping authority over the man. In this case, the wife is simply not under the authority of her husband. She is a law to herself and goes her own way. She refuses to live her life "out of the man," as I Corinthians 11:12 puts it. She does not seek to please the man,

The Christian Woman as Wife

as I Corinthians 7:34 teaches: "she that is married careth for the things of the world, how she may please her husband." She does not live as a help to her husband, this and this only, but as an independent person seeking her own things.

In both of these cases, the wife shows willful disregard for marriage as a divine institution. For the ground of the calling of the wife to submit and obey is the original institution of marriage by God. In the beginning, God created the man first and the woman second. He made the woman for the man, to be a help meet for him, not to be an independent person alongside of him. Added to this ground of wifely submission is the fact that the woman first fell into sin. This is taught by Paul in I Timothy 2:14. As another reason why the woman must not usurp authority over the man, he says: "And Adam was not deceived, but the woman being deceived was in the transgression." This reference by Paul to the woman's role in the Fall is fitting in the context of instruction concerning the woman's duty to be in subjection to the man. In the Fall, the wife erred in presenting herself as an independent power alongside her husband. She did this by virtue of the fact that she carried on a discussion with the serpent about God's prohibition of eating from the Tree of Knowledge. She should not have engaged in the discussion. God had given the man the commandment regarding the tree, not the woman. Genesis 3:2 should have read: "See my husband, serpent; he is my head, and I live only under him and out of him." Adam also erred by permitting his wife to get away with her usurpation of his authority. But God insisted on His ordinance: the authority of the man in marriage. For He came into the garden asking, "Adam, where are you?" He did not ask, "Eve, where are you?"

God gave the husband authority in the marriage bond, and God put the wife under that authority. Yes, *God did!* And still today, God maintains the original institution. Yes, *God does!* The wife is under her husband's authority: not a ruling head, but an obeying body. She is this whether she likes it or not, whether she lives that way or not. Now, the calling of the Christian woman as wife is: Honor the institution of marriage. Consciously, willingly agree to it; occupy that position; live that way. This is pleasing to God — not so much that you call your husband "honey" or "sweetheart," but that you call him "lord."

Basic to the willingness of a wife to be in subjection to her husband

> So I am supposed to be this shy girl who never talks - who does that?

FAR ABOVE RUBIES

is a sound mind. In the text in Titus, Paul twice uses the word that means "sound-minded." They are the words translated "sober" and "discreet." The young wives must be "sober" and "discreet," that is, sound-minded. The idea is that if the young wife has a sound mind she will submit to her husband and obey him; whereas if she entertains foolish thoughts she will not submit. The young wife is tempted to think foolishly about marriage, particularly about her calling in marriage, by the example of the unbelieving wives of the world. These women reject the fundamental virtue of the wife, submission. Especially in our time and in our society, they deny it and ridicule it. They claim that the wife is an equal partner in marriage. They insist that marriage is a contract between equals. There is, they say, no authority in this relationship, only mutual agreement. Also, they view the wife as basically independent of her husband. Although married, she has her own life, her own career, her own fulfillment as a woman, apart from her husband. In short, she is not and must not be considered to be a help meet for her husband.

These damnable lies have pernicious results. They are directly responsible for the appalling increase in broken marriages and homes, with all of the attendant misery and woe. No home that has two heads, or no head at all, can stand. Besides, where the authority of the husband over the wife is lacking, the authority of the parents over the children will invariably be lacking also, so that lawless parents spawn lawless children. These bitter consequences of the wife's rejection of her husband's authority are nothing else than God's judgment on those who despise His ordinance of marriage.

The example of the world is not the only temptation to the Christian wife. She herself has a sinful nature that is opposed to the calling to submit to her husband. By nature she is a rebel. According to her nature, she does not will to be in subjection to another, but to assert herself. She does not will to be the help of another, but to seek herself.

Over against the example of the world and over against your own nature now, be of a sound mind, says Paul. What is this sound mind? Essentially, it is the thinking of the young wife that considers how the church, the Bride, is related to Christ, her Husband, and how that church conducts herself toward Christ; then, it is the thinking that applies this great truth to her own marriage and to her own calling in

> Well I guess I'm a rebel. B/c I think there should be a head... the man - BUT the women also part of this marriage... should have a say. Definitly.

marriage. Marriage is the mystery of Christ and the church. So to regard marriage is to have a sound mind, that is, to be "sober" and "discreet." Just as the church submits to and obeys her Head, Jesus Christ, so you are to submit to your own husband and obey him. The church submits in everything. Nothing of her life falls outside the sphere of His authority. And the church obeys Christ even though the Lord requires hard things of her. Obedience to Christ often means loss, hardship, and even death for the church. Nor does the church live her life or any part of her life apart from Christ, in independence of Him. She has no life except her life in Christ. So the life of the Christian wife should be. *[handwritten: No life except in the husband? Just a lump?]*

This is not some great evil for the church. This is the blessedness, the true happiness, of the church. In the way of complete submission to Christ and in the way of living in Him, with Him, and out of Him, the church is blessed in time and eternity. So it is for the Christian wife. When God calls her to submit, He points out the way of happiness and life for her.

Young Christian wives must also be of a sound mind in their view of other important aspects of marriage. The text mentions them: their love for their own husbands, their love for their children, and their being "keepers at home." The Holy Spirit makes plain here that love is an essential element in the wife's calling. She must love her husband. The reason why Scripture stresses submission so strongly is not that Scripture minimizes love. In fact, the first and great commandment to the young wife is: Love your husband. Love is the fundamental virtue in marriage, also as regards the calling of the wife. Submission and obedience is the form that love takes in the case of the wife, the way that her love manifests itself. There can be no question about this in light of the great pattern of marriage. The basic characteristic of the relationship of the church to Christ is that the church loves Christ. In her love, she submits and obeys. Scripture does not minimize the importance of the wife's love, but it is concerned that this love will be genuine and that it will express itself and take form properly. And that form is submission!

In close connection with this concern, Scripture guards against a false romanticism concerning marriage to which young women are prone. Young women are inclined to dream of marriage as all emotional, passionate love, as a matter of moonlit nights and idyllic days. With such fantasies, they enter marriage. When they wake up to reality, they quickly desert and divorce. This is the view of marriage peddled by the world in its novels, its movies, and its television. In contrast, Scripture displays a matter-of-factness, a sober realism, about marriage that the Christian young woman should incorporate into her thinking before marriage and retain throughout her marriage. Not that Scripture destroys her idealism concerning marriage or is a foe of "romance." Have you never read the Song of Solomon? The estimation of marriage that regards it as nothing less than the mystery of Christ and the church insists on the highest idealism and opens the way to "romance" for every Christian marriage. But the Word of God gives the young women of the church the whole truth, so that they may have a sound mind. In marriage, they can expect children, the bearing and rearing of which will mean pain and sorrow. They must expect to be "keepers at home," or as a better translation has it, "workers at home." Theirs is not the glamour of the "career woman," but the patient, unsung, and often wearisome labor of the home and family. And even their love of their husband will not be an emotional, passionate, spontaneous thing, at least not entirely this, for the text teaches that this love for the husband is *taught* to the young wives by the older women. The aged women must "teach the young women to be sober, to love their husbands." If the older women teach this love, the young wives must *learn* this love. This is arduous, spiritual activity; for the husband, although a Christian, will soon prove himself to be no "prince charming," but a very weak and sinful man, whom it is not always easy to love.

If these characteristics of a wife are the product of a sound mind, it is evident that the world is mad. The women of the world in our day are fools, diseased of mind, walking "in the vanity of their mind, having the understanding darkened, being alienated from the life of God through the ignorance that is in them, because of the blindness of their heart," as Paul says in Ephesians 4:17, 18. For they do the very opposite of the requirements of our text. They do not love their own husbands, but they love many men, whether simultaneously in adultery or successively by divorce and remarriage. This is the sin par excellence against the command of God to be submissive to one's own husband.

To forsake one's husband and to live with another man is the most extreme form of rebellion and disobedience. These vile creatures hate the very thought of children and in their hatred for their own children murder them before they can see the light of day. If a child comes in spite of their precautions, they regard him as a hindrance and a bother, ignore him, and farm him out as quickly as possible to nursery school and baby-sitters. According to these women, true happiness is not to be found in the activity of a wife and the activity of a "worker at home." This is drudgery and slavery from which they must be liberated. They seek happiness in a career, a job outside the home, or in gadding about.

In contrast to this madness, let the Christian wife have a sound mind. Know the truth about your calling, not from magazines and novels but from Holy Scripture. Take as your examples, not the wretched heroines of television, but holy Sarah and the other saintly women. Consider what God says about wives, marital faithfulness, children, housewifery, and obedience. God's Word — on this subject also — is the truth. It is the highest wisdom. Here, too, the wisdom of the world is mere foolishness, nothing more. God's Word calls the Christian woman to a work that is of the greatest worth. The life of the young woman described in the text is not drudgery. On the contrary, her life is glorious and her labor is important. "Who can find a virtuous woman? for her price is far above rubies. The heart of her husband doth safely trust in her.... She will do him good and not evil.... She looketh well to the ways of her household, and eateth not the bread of idleness.... Many daughters have done virtuously, but thou excellest them all" (Prof. 31:10-31). Even the angels of heaven are not so glorious, nor their work so important.

Only a God-fearing young woman can and will fulfill this high calling. This is why Proverbs 31 concludes its description of the virtuous woman by saying, "Favour is deceitful, and beauty is vain: but a woman that feareth the Lord, she shall be praised" (vs. 30). Doing the duty of a wife is simply a matter of fearing the Lord. This is true, first of all, of the calling of the wife to be in subjection to her husband. It is God's authority that is vested in the husband. Whether or not a wife will call her husband "lord," therefore, depends on whether or not she calls God "Lord." Her reverence for her husband depends on her reverence for God. The Christian wife is motivated to carry out her calling by her fear of the Lord God. She does not do it for her husband's sake, her children's sake, or her own sake, but for the Lord's sake. She behaves herself as a good wife so that she may thus show her thankfulness to God for His salvation of her and so that He may be praised by her, particularly by her reflection in her married life of the behavior of the church toward Christ. Therefore, although her husband may be unappreciative, often derelict in his own duty, and even an unbeliever, the Christian wife faithfully and joyfully continues in her calling.

An implication of this for the believing young man is that he must make this the all-important question as he looks for a wife: Does she fear God? May he believe, and not have to find out by bitter experience, that favor is deceitful and beauty, vain.

To a God-fearing wife it is important that God's Word not be blasphemed, especially that it not be blasphemed on account of her. This is what the text holds before the Christian wife as her purpose for heeding her calling. She must love her husband, love her children, work at home, and be submissive, "so that the word of God be not blasphemed." There is a close, inseparable connection between the Word of God which we confess as Christians and our conduct in the world. If we walk wickedly, we bring reproach upon the Word of God. When we walk uprightly, by the power of the Word itself, we bring praise upon the Word of God, for in this case we are doing "the things which become sound doctrine" (2:1). When the world sees a wife who professes Christ Jesus living insolently and evilly over against her husband, not only do they mock her and her marriage, but they also speak evil of the Word of God which the wife confesses. She gives occasion to the world to hold God's Word in contempt, as if it did not possess the power to make any real difference in the life of God's people or as if the Word of God tolerated a rebellious wife. If nothing else touches you, let this move you to heed your calling as a wife. The fact that God's Word is blasphemed by the bad behavior of a wife implies that God's Word is praised by her good behavior. Even the world must glorify God when they see Christian wives living with their husbands in accordance with the text. These are powerful motives for a believing woman. She detests all blasphemy of God and His Word. She loves to have God's Word praised. Compelled by these incentives, the God-fearing woman will be submissive and sound-minded.

The marriage of the Christian man who dwells with his wife according to knowledge and the Christian woman who submits and is sound-minded is a glorious and delightful thing. In starkest contrast to it stand the marriages of the world. In the world, marriage is the battlefield on which a vicious, relentless struggle rages between the tyrant-husband and the rebel-wife. Now the one, now the other is temporarily victorious. At present, in our society, the rebellious woman has the upper hand. If the world lasts, the male will again assert himself, overthrow the woman's dominance, and rule her more tyrannically than before. The Christian marriage is radically different. The husband rules in love. The wife submits in love. Marriage, thus, is not a framework for bitterest strife and mutual destruction, but a relationship of fellowship, joy, and mutual help. There is peace.

This is possible! This is expected! This is our calling! For it belongs to the great salvation of the sovereign grace of God in Jesus Christ.

You husbands and wives, pray this without doubting. Work to realize this, to the glory of God's Word — and your own happiness.

The Hope of the Covenant Mother in the Old Dispensation

Cornelius Hanko

Throughout the ages the hope of godly mothers has been the blessing of bringing forth the children of the covenant. Scripture emphasizes this truth especially in the Old Testament. In a speech delivered at the League of Ladies' Societies in the First Protestant Reformed Church of Grand Rapids, Michigan, Rev. Cornelius Hanko points out how the examples of covenant mothers serve as an inspiration to mothers of new dispensational times as well. This speech was delivered in 1948, long before the Reformed church world was troubled by the question of the role of women in the church. Rev. Hanko is emeritus minister of Hudsonville Protestant Reformed Church in Hudsonville, Michigan.The Hope of the Covenant Mother in the Old Dispensation

The Hope of the Covenant Mother in the Old Dispensation

The birth of a child is often hailed as "a blessed event." Sometimes this is meant in all seriousness, but often it carries a ring of irony in it. In a world of sinful men who are filled with "the lust of the flesh, the lust of the eyes and the pride of life," children are often considered a burden and even a nuisance. Some would even hesitate about bringing a new generation into the miseries of an earthly existence. The anticipation of motherhood and the stigma of a large family are frequently looked upon with dread. Yet the fact remains that from the very dawn of history believing women were thrilled with the joy that belongs peculiarly to a real mother. This is not simply because of the motherly instinct of the woman nor because the child makes the family unit complete and brings happiness into the home. But the real reason why a believing mother rejoices in the birth of her child is that she thereby realizes her purpose in the covenant according to the will of God.

This is especially evident from the church of the old dispensation where it was a source of constant grief to many believing women that they were deprived of the joy of motherhood. They realized that only in the line of continued generations could the Christ, the hope of their salvation, be born. All their salvation was wrapped up in the promised seed. All God's promises centered in Him. They were blessed in bringing forth that seed. For their hope was fixed upon the word of the Lord that was spoken to Satan immediately after the fall, "I will put enmity between thee and the woman, and between thy seed and her seed; it shall bruise thy head, and thou shalt bruise his heel."

It is interesting to trace that hope of the believing mothers of the Old Testament through a few of its outstanding phases.

Notice, first of all, the case of Eve, the mother of all the living. When she brought forth her firstborn son into the world, she exclaimed, "I have gotten a man from the Lord." No doubt, she was filled with the amazement of any mother who gives birth to a child. No one can help but marvel at the wonder that has taken place. Here you have a well formed individual with eyes and ears and nose and mouth, with hands that wave and feet that kick, with lungs that breathe in perfect rhythm, a heart that beats, and a stomach that demands its food at regular intervals. It bears the likeness of father or mother, or more likely of both. It has its own features, its own characteristics, its own nature, its own place in the family, in the church, and in the midst of this world. It has a spiritual existence whereby it lives its life before the face of God and finally passes on into eternity. It is a man or a woman in miniature, that will take its own place and serve its own purpose in life.

But surely Eve saw more than that in her first child. She realized that hereby God's purpose was being realized, that man should "be fruitful, and multiply and replenish the earth." This child was the first of the family the Lord would give them. He was a concrete evidence of the race that was to be born.

Yet considering that through the fall Adam and Eve had a depraved nature, she also must realize that her children were conceived and born in sin. Despair might have drowned every joy at the thought of bringing forth a carnal seed that was prone to all evil. How evident that became in the later history of Cain, for he slew his righteous brother Abel and became a vagabond upon the earth. We can well imagine what a grief this son caused his parents, especially when they realized that he had received his sinful nature from them as a result of their fall. But Eve was able to look beyond these things, for to her was promised a seed that would crush the head of the serpent. That hope flooded her soul as she took her firstborn son into her arms. Did she imagine that this child might already be the promised Savior? We can only surmise. Yet this is certain, that when she exclaimed, "I have gotten a man from the Lord," she gave expression to all the hope that lived in her heart.

Then there is the case of Sarah, whose daughters ye are when ye walk in her faith (I Pet. 3:6). As you know, God called Abraham out of Ur of the Chaldees to bring him to the land of Canaan, that he might become the father of all believers. To him came the promise, "I will establish my covenant between me and thee and thy seed after thee, in their generations for an everlasting covenant, to be a God unto thee, and to thy seed after thee." Yet, strange as it may seem, God had given to Abraham a wife who from a natural aspect saw the hopes of motherhood vanish as the years rolled by, for she was barren. She had grown old, so that she was like a dead corpse as far as the prospects of becoming a mother were concerned. To give birth to a child now had definitely become a human impossibility. It seems utterly hopeless that the promised seed could ever be born from her. Yet all the salvation of the world was wrapped up in that seed. If she would die childless, the Christ could not come and God's promise would fail. God would not be God, for He would prove unfaithful to His word.

That accounts for it that she conceived of the plot to employ her slave Hagar for the purpose of producing the desired seed. After conferring with Abraham on the matter, it was agreed that this might prove to be a way out of their difficulty, so that the impossible might still come to pass. We should note that Abraham and Sarah had no intention of allowing Hagar to lay any claim to her own child. She was to serve as a slave, a bondwoman, to her mistress, to supply her mistress with a child. Sarah would claim the child which was born to her from Abraham through the bondwoman, and she would present this child to God as a possible heir of the promise.

We know that the plot failed miserably. God had no need of Sarah's scheming to realize His promise. The incident brought untold grief in the house of Abraham. But the outcome was that God proved that He could do that which was impossible with man. He performs the wonder of His grace, bringing forth the living from the dead.

We need only mention in passing Rebekah, the wife of Isaac. She also was barren. It looked as if Isaac had made a mistake after all in taking Rebekah to wife, for she was unable to bring forth the seed out of which the Christ should be born. Would the hopes of Abraham and Sarah still perish? But the Lord heard her prayer, so that she anticipated the birth of twins. And yet, before the children were born the Lord made plain to her that the sword of election and reprobation would pass between her offspring, for the one, even the firstborn, would have no part whatever in God's covenant. Not in Esau, but in Jacob lay the hope of the coming of the Christ and the ingathering of God's church.

And finally, not to mention any more, we pause at the example of Hannah, the mother of Samuel. Scripture informs us that she was the beloved wife of Elkanah, yet she also was barren. It is certainly significant that there were so many barren women in the line of the covenant in the old dispensation. It plainly reveals that the church is born, not of him who willeth, nor of him who runneth, but of God who showeth mercy.

We are all acquainted with Hannah's prayer for a child, the Lord's answer to her prayer, and the fact that she dedicated this child to the Lord in the tabernacle at Shiloh. Her request was certainly unique. Plainly she was not simply interested in being relieved of the stigma of her barrenness. Nor was she interested in brightening her home with a child. She was governed by entirely different considerations. She requests a child, but only with certain definite stipulations. First of all, it must be a male child. A daughter would not serve her purpose. Moreover, it must be a child which the Lord will receive as a Nazarite from birth, to be devoted to the tabernacle and to the Lord all the days of his life. Finally this implies that it must be a true covenant seed. She has no need for a carnal seed, but this child must serve the very definite purpose of delivering Israel from all her troubles.

Hannah's prayer arises from the heart of a true mother in Israel. No wonder that her song of thanksgiving is prophetic of the Song of Mary. Years later the mother of Jesus takes up this song of Hannah as she realizes that she is the most blessed among women, the one in whom all the hopes of the covenant mothers of the old dispensation were fulfilled.

* * * * * * *

Thus far we have noticed that the hope of the believing women in the old dispensation centered on the promised Christ. When sin entered into the world God promised salvation through the Seed that would be born. Fallen mankind lay in the midst of death, sold under sin, with no escape except for that promised Seed, the Christ. Out of the natural, carnal seed that would be born to our first parents God would take unto Himself a spiritual seed, an elect generation, the church. And in the line of generations of this spiritual seed the Christ would be born. Thus the hope of the believing mother was fixed upon that promised Christ. She longed to have a part in bringing Him forth and thus see her promise realized. She was blessed in bearing children, for therein lay the hope of her salvation.

We have traced that hope as it lived in the hearts of some of the believing women, particularly in Eve, Sarah, Rebekah, and Hannah.

But we cannot fail to note that this hope was always accompanied by an intense struggle. Without a bitter, life-long struggle that hope could never be realized, even according to the divine purpose.

The Hope of the Covenant Mother

The Lord Himself occasions that struggle. He creates a twofold seed in the line of the generations of the human race. He establishes enmity between them, and by the way of struggle causes the Christ-Child to be born, who destroys the power of Satan and gives His people the eternal victory.

We should not fail to note, first of all, that even within the church there is always a reprobate, carnal seed as well as an elect, spiritual seed. There are always dead branches in the true Vine as it manifests itself here on earth. There are still good and bad fishes in the net of God's covenant as it sweeps through the sea of this world. There is chaff as well as wheat in the harvest as long as it still stands upon the field. There is scaffolding as well as the building proper as long as God's Temple is under construction. It is not all Israel that is called Israel.

Secondly, it is worthy of note that the natural seed is always first and serves to bring forth the spiritual. Even in nature the straw serves to produce the kernel of wheat, so that finally the chaff and the straw are burned, but the wheat is gathered into the granary. So also God gathers His church from the natural seed that is born in the line of the continued generations of believers. And finally we must note that the natural, carnal seed is always in the majority and is always stronger than the spiritual seed, when viewed from the earthly aspect. The carnal element holds the position of power even within the church as it manifests itself here on earth. It always opposes the spiritual element and seeks to destroy it. It persecutes the believers, crucifies the Christ, and in every way proudly exalts itself against the Lord and His Anointed. The heathen rage furiously and the peoples imagine vain things even in the domain of the covenant. For the Lord has placed enmity between the devil and the woman, between the seed of the devil and the seed of the woman, until finally the seed of the woman crushes the head of the devil to powder, even while he is busy bruising its heel.

That is quite evident from the examples we cited previously.

Notice again the exultant cry of the mother of all living when she took up her firstborn son and said, "I have gotten a man of the Lord." We could well imagine that she was bitterly disillusioned when later she realized that this son was simply a product of her own sinful flesh, the seed of the serpent. Cain was the firstborn, and therefore Eve readily built her hopes upon that child. Moreover, he was evidently the picture of strength and comeliness. When Abel was born she calls him `breath,' `vanity,' for he must have been a puny child, upon whom was plainly written the sad results of their fall. Yet according to the will and purpose of God, Cain was the reprobate seed. That became evident as he grew up under the covenant training of his God-fearing parents. Cain revealed only animosity over against all the evidences of God's grace in the life of Abel. Even Cain's sacrifice was a wicked product of his own abominable self-righteousness. Finally Cain reveals his true nature by killing Abel in a vain desire to wipe out God's church. But Cain does serve his purpose. He was the firstborn son, and therefore proof of the fact that God would give them a seed. And at the same time he opened the way for that true seed as it was represented in Abel. Therefore the exuberant joy of Eve at the birth of her firstborn was certainly not in vain. It did express her hope of the fulfillment of the promise of God, even though she had still to learn by sad experience that this hope would be realized only by way of struggle.

Then we have the history of Sarah in connection with the birth of Ishmael from Hagar. Many have regarded Hagar as a victim of the capricious whims of Sarah. In fact, Sarah is often condemned for her bitterness toward Ishmael, for demanding that he be sent out of the house, and for insisting that he be disowned as Abraham's heir. For that is what happens. After the Lord makes plain to Sarah that she herself shall have a son in her old age, and that Isaac shall be the promised seed, Sarah becomes increasingly more determined that Hagar and her son shall not abide under their roof. The day even arrives that Abraham is forced to send the bondwoman and her son away emptyhanded.

But before we criticize Sarah we must bear in mind that Scripture takes her side in the matter. God demands of Abraham that he comply with her wishes, for the son of the bondwoman must not inherit with the son of the free (Gal. 4). The facts in the case are these: when Hagar realized that she would bear Abraham a son, she proudly despised her mistress. According to her estimation, not Sarah, but *she* was the covenant mother, the real wife of Abraham. Had not God privileged her above Sarah? Therefore she was also determined to claim her own child. She would never give it up to her mistress. That accounts for her

The Hope of the Covenant Mother

insubordination to Sarah and her fleeing away. And that also takes into account the fact that the Lord insists that she must return to her mistress and submit to her until the child is born, for the Lord will see to it that in due time she may claim her own child. Later Hagar even impresses upon Ishmael's mind that he is the firstborn, and therefore the rightful heir. That is the reason why Ishmael mocks with Isaac, over whom they make such an undue fuss. The son of the bondwoman, Abraham's natural seed, proudly exalts and maintains himself over against the child of the promise, with the result that God Himself requires that the haughty rebel be cast out of the house in which he has no rightful claim. After a bitter struggle it becomes evident to all that the purpose according to election must stand, for "in Isaac shall thy seed be called."

We can pass over the struggle in Isaac's family with but a few words. Before the twins were ever born, Isaac and Rebekah were informed that the knife of divine election and reprobation had cut sharply between them. They were even given to understand that the firstborn, Esau, would have no part in the covenant whatsoever. Sovereign election centered upon Jacob; reprobation rested on Esau. Rebekah proves to be able to adjust herself to this awful revelation more readily than Isaac. He favors the firstborn and even plays with the idea that he might still be the covenant seed. From a purely natural point of view it is not difficult for us to place ourselves in his position, since Esau was his own flesh and blood and had a natural appeal besides, so that Isaac did not like to see him perish. Yet Isaac is wrong, and learned to realize it only after failing in a final desperate attempt to place the blessing upon him. But then he is also ready to declare blessed him whom God will bless.

This throws light on the history of Hannah. She also experienced the struggle within her own household. Hannah was barren, so that her husband Elkanah foolishly devised the plot to take Peninnah to wife, in order that she might serve to bring the joys of the covenant mother into Hannah's life. In this attempt Elkanah fails miserably. For Peninnah is carnal, even as Hannah is deeply spiritual. She readily usurps Hannah's place as Elkanah's wife, and scornfully mocks with Hannah particularly because she is able to present Elkanah with children. That drove Hannah to a point where she pours out her soul in prayer to the Lord at Shiloh. It was an ominous time. These were the days when there was no king in Israel and every man did that which was right in his own eyes. The carnal seed had the upper hand, not only in Hannah's home, but even in all Israel, so that corruption was rampant even to the tabernacle at Shiloh. The spiritual seed was being oppressed, even threatened with destruction. Therefore she prays, not merely for a child, especially not more carnal seed, but for one who can be a Samuel, an "answered of the Lord," to cleanse the sanctuary and to preserve God's church upon the earth. She wants a son whom she may dedicate as a devoted servant to the Lord all the days of his life, that Israel may thus be preserved and that the Christ may come.

Hannah and the whole church of the old dispensation saw their hope fulfilled in Mary, the most blessed among women. With her they lift up their voice in triumph saying, "For unto us a Child is born, unto us a Son is given: and the government shall be upon His shoulders: and His name shall be called Wonderful, Counsellor, The Mighty God, The Everlasting Father, The Prince of Peace."

By way of struggle the hope of the believer is realized. How could it be otherwise? For God's promise never fails. By a wonder of grace He gathers His own in the continued line of believers. He transforms natural, carnal, even depraved sons of wrath into spiritual children of the kingdom of heaven. And He sends His own Son into the flesh, conceived by the Holy Ghost, born of the virgin Mary. He is God's Son, yet born in our likeness, son of Eve, son of Sarah, son of Rebekah, son of Ruth, son of Mary; Immanuel, God with us! God proves that nothing is impossible with Jehovah our covenant God.

These things are written for our example.

This same hope still lives in the hearts of the believers in the new dispensation. Believing mothers still exultingly say with the mother of all living, "I have gotten a man of the Lord." We can readily understand that a world steeped in iniquity refuses to be burdened with the anxieties of child-birth and the trouble of rearing a family. And why bring more children into the misery of this world? It is even an evidence of unbelief within the church that many will follow the same reasonings as the world and resort to the same practices to satisfy the lusts of the flesh without becoming involved in a family. The carnal element within the church is a friend of the world even in that respect. But the true covenant mother counts herself blessed in receiving children from the

The Hope of the Covenant Mother

Lord. In her own small way she is instrumental in bringing forth God's church and establishing His kingdom. She considers it only a wonder of divine grace that she herself may know the Lord. That wonder is only enriched by the fact that she is privileged to have children who fear the Lord and walk in His ways. She sees even in that the answer to her prayer "Thy kingdom come."

But this hope is never realized without a struggle, also today. The carnal seed is still always in the majority and lords it over the spiritual seed. It still seeks to destroy God's church. Therefore we are called to wage an untiring battle. We must be spiritually strong, arraying ourselves as the party of the living God against the powers of darkness. We must be ready at all times to give account of the hope that is within us. We must hold firmly to the truth entrusted unto us, that no man may take our crown. It is our calling to pass on to the generations to come the glorious heritage of truth which was delivered over to us from the fathers. That calls for covenant training in the home, in the church, and in the school, based entirely upon the Word of God.

The outcome is always safe with God. For we shall finally appear before Him with the church of all ages, saying, "Behold us, Lord, and the children which Thou hast given us, for they are Thine."

May that hope never grow dim among us.

Children in Marriage

David J. Engelsma

The purpose of marriage is, among other things, the bringing forth of children. Specifically, in the line of God's covenant, the purpose of marriage is to bring forth the children of the covenant. The important role which children play in the realization of God's covenant is addressed in this chapter, also taken from Prof. Engelsma's book *Marriage: The Mystery of Christ and the Church.*

Children in Marriage

And God blessed them, and God said unto them, Be fruitful, and multiply, and replenish the earth, and subdue it: and have dominion over the fish of the sea, and over the fowl of the air, and over every living thing that moveth upon the earth.
Genesis 1:28

Unto the woman he said, I will greatly multiply thy sorrow and thy conception; in sorrow thou shalt bring forth children; and thy desire shall be to thy husband, and he shall rule over thee.
Genesis 3:16

Notwithstanding she shall be saved in childbearing, if they continue in faith and charity and holiness with sobriety.
I Timothy 2:15

At the present time, there is a furor in both the world and the churches over birth control. The Roman Catholic Church is in an uproar over this issue. It has been the teaching of Rome in the past that the practice of birth control by artificial or mechanical means is grave sin. Pope after pope has plainly and emphatically taught this in official documents, or encyclicals. For this reason it is surprising that there is as much amazement at the present pope's teaching, and opposition to it, as there is. His is no new teaching in any respect. Besides, contradiction of the teachings of former popes would jeopardize Rome's doctrine of papal infallibility.

In the past few years, at the insistence of many Roman Catholics, the question of birth control was restudied. Recently, the pope issued an encyclical called ***Humanae Vitae*** (the English title is: "On the Regulation of Birth"), in which he fully supported Rome's historic teaching regarding birth control and condemned as grave sin every act of birth prevention. Since then a storm of protest has raged in the Roman church, threatening to some extent even the supremacy of the pope. The world has involved itself in Rome's struggle. Editorialists, educators, social agencies, and even government officials criticize Rome's position. Many were angered by the pope's decision because a project is under way at the present time to limit births on a worldwide scale. The pope's decision, it is feared, will hinder these efforts. Inevitably, the Protestant leaders had something to say. They condemned the Roman doctrine almost unanimously. Most of Protestantism advocates birth control as godly behavior and condemns the failure to practice it as immoral.

This entire question, and the controversy that surrounds it, affects us. The issue is out in the open. The practice itself of birth control becomes a problem for believing husbands and wives. The question is raised: What must the attitude of the Christian husband and wife be toward birth control?

Not only are the standards by which we judge the issue, and the conclusions to which we come, different from the standards and conclusions of the world, but the very point of view with which we consider the issue is different. The underlying issue, and fundamental question, for us is: What is the place of children in marriage? Bearing and rearing children is an aspect of the reality of marriage. Since marriage from beginning to end is a divine institution, not our thinking, but God's will is determinative for our behavior in marriage, also as regards having or not having children. Therefore, we look to God's Word, the Holy Scriptures, for the answer to the basic question: What is the place of children in the marriage of believers?

* * * * * * *

Erroneous explanations of the place of children in marriage have been found in the church. These are explanations that err by overemphasizing the importance of children in marriage. Perhaps the exaggeration is due to men's feeling that they have to fight very vehemently against the prevalent disparagement of children. Whatever the motive, such exaggerations are harmful. They thoughtlessly injure some of God's people — for example, the childless couple — and they do damage to the truth of marriage itself. These exaggerations ascribe one purpose to marriage, namely, having children, and virtually deny the completeness and worth of marriage apart from children.

Those who preach such notions probably suppose that they are stressing the importance of children; in fact, they are denying the significance of marriage. A marriage between a man and a woman is complete in itself. For marriage in its deepest significance is the symbol of the relationship of love and fellowship between Christ and the church. When a believing man and his believing wife live together in love, according to the pattern of Christ and His Bride, God's highest purpose with marriage is realized, even though there are no children in the marriage. Although God may withhold children from a married couple, the husband and the wife have during all their life important and demanding work to do. They have the lofty calling of showing forth the mystery of Christ and the church. They have the high calling of fulfilling the mutual responsibilities of husband and wife in their life together.

Closely related to the error of making marriage depend on children is the assertion that the only legitimate use of sex is the begetting of children. Undoubtedly, the reason for such a statement is fear of the trend today to sunder sex and procreation. But Scripture makes clear that the sexual relationship between a man and his wife has a purpose and value other than that of begetting children. It is an aspect of the amazing and joyful intimacy of marriage and an expression of the unique relationship of love in marriage. It is an important part of marriage's fellowship.

With this use of the sexual relationship, however, God has mingled another use, namely, the begetting of children. The two purposes of God with regard to sex in marriage have been joined together very closely. In the practice of birth control, man separates, or tries to separate, what God has joined together. Man tries to retain the expression and enjoyment of the intimacy of marriage, while excluding the bringing forth of children. At once, the question arises: Does man have the right to do this? May he so separate the two uses of the sexual relationship? In addition, the question arises, whether man can really do this. Of course, we know that man today, with his pills and devices, can effectively prevent the conception of a child. But does he retain the intimacy, the fellowship? There is some fear today that certain means of birth control are dangerous because they adversely affect the mysterious make-up and workings of the body. There is at least as much reason to fear that man's tampering with sex, in the interest of frustrating one of the functions God has given it, namely, the begetting of children, adversely affects the mysterious make-up and workings of the souls of a man and his wife and thus hinders the intimacy of the marital relationship, as well as the procreative aspect.

For us, God's Word is decisive. Between us and the world there is a radical difference as regards our view of marriage. It is not the case that basically we both have the same view of marriage but that we differ only on certain details of married life. Rather, we have fundamentally different views of marriage. The difference is between a God-centered view of marriage and a man-centered view. For unbelievers, marriage begins and ends with themselves: their happiness, their pleasure, their comfort, and their will. Our marriages, however, begin and end with God. Our marriages are not ultimately for our sake, but for God's sake; they are not for our ease and pleasure, but they are in the service of God's purpose and for His honor. Our marriages are *His* in the fullest sense. Right behavior in marriage, therefore, consists of submitting to God's will as He makes it known in His Word. We may not answer the hard questions of married life by considering how we ourselves think or feel at the moment, but we must look to God's Word for His will. Then, even though painfully at times, we must again and again bring our wills into conformity with His.

God's Word speaks of child-bearing and the place of children in marriage at three distinct stages of human history. These three stages are represented in the three texts that are quoted above: Genesis 1:28, Genesis 3:16, and I Timothy 2:15. These texts teach us the place of children in marriage according to God's original institution in Paradise before the Fall; the effect of the Fall on child-bearing; and the significance of childbearing for believing women in the church today.

Genesis 1:28 is the powerful Word of God to the just-created man and his wife which bestows on them the gift of sex and which commands them to bring forth children by it. "And God blessed them, and God said unto them, Be fruitful, and multiply, and replenish the earth, and subdue it: and have dominion over the fish of the sea, and over the fowl of the air, and over every living thing that moveth upon the earth." As given originally, the sexual relation in marriage has as a divine purpose fruitfulness and multiplying, that is, the bringing forth of children. This was God's will with it "from the beginning," and God made this purpose of begetting children something inherent in sex itself. The goal of Adam and Eve's bringing forth children was man's exercising dominion over all the earth. Adam and Eve alone could not do this; full dominion over the earthly creation demanded a race of godly kings and queens.

Genesis 3:16 instructs us that our Fall into sin affected motherhood and childbearing. We read: "Unto the woman he said, I will greatly multiply thy sorrow and thy conception; in sorrow thou shalt bring forth children; and thy desire shall be to thy husband, and he shall rule over thee." This text speaks of the chastisement which God inflicted on the woman because of her part in the Fall. The idea is that there will be hardships that God brings into the life of all women generally. From now on, enduring these hardships will be part of the life of woman. What concerns us is that the chastisement was an increase of the woman's conception of children and an increase of sorrow on the woman's part as regards this conception. In other words, the woman will conceive children more frequently than she would have before the Fall. Also, she will bring forth these children in sorrow. This sorrow of child-bearing does not refer only to the physical pain at the time of delivery, although this by itself would be severe, but it also refers to the physical pain that often accompanies carrying the child before birth and to the physical hardships that a mother endures as she rears her children. However, the sorrow of child-bearing does not refer exclusively to physical pain and hardship. The bitterest sorrow of all is the sorrow of bearing and rearing sinful children. Think of the grief of Mother Eve as she watched her firstborn son grow up a godless, unbelieving man; and think of her sorrow as she buried a son whose life was cut off in youth by the hand of his own brother, her son.

The Scriptures also speak of the motherhood of regenerated women. This sheds light on another distinct aspect of the truth of children in marriage. In I Timothy 2:15, after Paul has noted that it was the woman who was deceived and who first sinned in Paradise, he says: "Notwithstanding she shall be saved in childbearing, if they continue in faith and charity and holiness with sobriety." Such is the importance of childbearing that, as a rule, it is the way in which God saves believing women.

It is clear from all these passages of Scripture that begetting and bearing children is the will of God. He made it an integral part of marriage in the beginning. He imposed the painful aspects of child-bearing on woman after the Fall. He sanctifies childbearing in the church, so that it is a way of salvation for believing women. But what we must see in these passages above all is that child-bearing is a *blessing* to us. In the beginning, God blessed Adam and Eve with fruitfulness:

"And God blessed them, and God said, ... Be fruitful" (Gen. 1:28). Fruitfulness in marriage was a good thing. Nor did child-bearing, as such, become a curse after the Fall. Although we read that God cursed the serpent and that God cursed the ground for man's sake, we do not read that God cursed Eve when He imposed on her the hardships of motherhood. The sorrows attending conception were chastisements for her, not a curse. Besides, it was not child-bearing itself that was inflicted on the woman after the Fall but an increase of child-bearing and an increase of sorrow. That child-bearing is a blessing of God in Christ to believing women is strongly emphasized by Paul in I Timothy 2:15. It is now a way of salvation for them. This then is our view of children in our marriages: children are a blessing.

The view of the world is radically different. Underlying all of the world's arguments in favor of birth prevention is the conviction that child-bearing and children are a curse. This is the heart of the issue regarding birth control: Are children a blessing or a curse? The world has certain grounds for its contention that children are a curse, but these grounds are flimsy and certainly do not weigh with God's people. The world screams for birth control because of a "population explosion" which may cause famine. Even if this were so, the danger of a famine is not in our country, where it is played up, but in countries like India. In our country, parents are more capable of supporting large families financially than people ever have been before. Our land is capable of supplying an abundance of luxuries, much more than the bare needs of its people. A country that spends scores of billions of dollars to go to the moon, that spends billions of dollars for a war in Vietnam, that has much of its farm land in the soil bank, and that wastes its resources as prodigally as ours does is not even worthy of a hearing when it tells us to limit our families because of a shortage of natural resources. The world also makes a feeble attempt to support its program of birth prevention by suggesting that fewer children are better reared. But the falsity of this claim is proved by our society. In our society, among those whose citizenship is in this world, it seems to be a rule that the fewer the children, the less attention paid to them and the worse their rearing.

These are the world's arguments, based on the world's thinking and geared to the world's goals. All of them are man-centered. They appeal to man's desire for luxuries — luxuries which a large family might have to forgo. They appeal to the woman's desire to have much time for herself, which is impossible if she has many children. Let us confess it, they find a ready response in our flesh also: children, especially many children, are a bother and a nuisance, because they interfere with our fun and games.

God is not in all the world's thoughts on the matter of "family planning." They know no Sovereign, Lord of heaven and earth, who regulates births according to an all-wise counsel. They have no heavenly Father upon whom to depend for daily bread. We must not be influenced by the world's arguments, nor may we adopt their viewpoint. There may be too many worldlings on earth, but are there too many children of God? God's purpose with children in the beginning was that there be a race of godly kings who subject the creation to Him. Today, because of God's covenant of grace in Jesus Christ, God realizes this purpose in the children of believers. This is the way we should look at the number of people on earth.

We should also fortify ourselves against the State's illegitimate intrusion into this aspect of our lives. The State has no authority to dictate the size of our families. At the present, the State subjects us to moral pressure in order to make us limit our families to 2.3 children. But already the State begins to make threatening noises about penalizing those who have more children than it permits. The time may very well come when the State demands obedience to its law regulating the size of families. As Christians, we are bound to provide for our families, to rear them well, and to train our children to work; but we are not bound to obey any law that decrees the number of children we may have. Over against the State's will that we not bear children stands the will of God expressed by Paul in I Timothy 5:14: "I will therefore that the younger women marry, bear children, guide the house, give none occasion to the adversary to speak reproachfully."

There is one hard aspect of child-bearing that does weigh heavily with the church. This is the sorrow of motherhood. There is the physical toil and pain of giving birth and of rearing the children. There is also the labor and sorrow of the mother's soul as she carries out this calling. The sorrow of motherhood is great! According to Genesis 3:16, God greatly multiplied the woman's sorrow and conception, so that the sorrow in which she brings forth children is a great sorrow. In a certain sense, the mother must give her life away for the sake of the children. This is the burden of the woman, because of sin. Nor does God bless the motherhood of a believing woman by removing all the hardships and making motherhood easy in her case. God does bless her as a mother, but not in this way. The burden of sorrow and the burden of the increase of pregnancy remain also for her.

But what now is the "solution" for the believing woman? Where does her salvation lie? Is the answer this, that she evade the burden by refusing to have children; or is the answer this, that she find grace and strength in Jesus Christ to bear the burden of motherhood? The unbelieving women of the world simply evade the burden by preventing the birth of children. They reject motherhood with its great sorrow. They seek "fulfillment" outside the home in other vocations. Generally speaking, however, there has never been a more troubled, dissatisfied, unhappy, and ungodly woman than the modern "emancipated" American woman. This psychological and spiritual wretchedness bears out what Paul wrote in I Timothy 2:15: "She shall be saved in [literally: "through"] childbearing."

Motherhood is hard. But the answer for women who profess godliness is not to escape it, as is possible today. For she is *saved* by child-bearing. The apostle certainly means the spiritual salvation of Christ crucified and risen. Ordinarily, the eternal salvation of the believing woman is tied up with child-bearing. It is not the case that the woman enjoys salvation for the first time when she bears a child. Neither is it so, that child-bearing itself saves in any sense. The text shows this when it adds: "if they continue in faith and charity and holiness and sobriety." Rather, child-bearing is ordinarily the way, the earthly way of life, in which God saves believing women in the sense of maintaining their salvation and enriching it.

The believing woman, therefore, faced with the sorrows of motherhood, must respond, not by avoiding this difficult way, but by seeking the grace of Christ to endure the sorrows and to perform the labor. And the church, sympathetic toward the sorrows of the "mothers in Israel," does not begin to preach the worldly wisdom of "family planning." But she strengthens and comforts with the Word of God. She directs mothers to the strong and compassionate Savior, Jesus

Christ, whose grace is sufficient for all their burdens. He knows the great sorrows of motherhood. He Himself grew up in a family of at least seven children and possibly more. Matthew 13:55, 56 informs us that Jesus had four brothers and at least two sisters. He knows by experience the needs of mothers with large families, having seen these needs in His own beloved mother. He is able to give grace to help in time of need.

Christ strengthens and gladdens parents in the church by proclaiming in His Word that He saves their children. God's covenant with His people, as well today as in Old Testament times, includes as a precious element that God will be the God of our children after us. On the very day of the dawning of the new dispensation, when God's church had come to maturity, the Holy Spirit had Peter cry out: "For the promise is unto you, and to your children" (Acts 2:39). Thus, we find throughout the New Testament that the children of believers are included in the church as members (Eph. 6:1-4; Col. 3:20, 21).

Christ builds up His church from our children. He makes our children kings, who not only will rule with Him everlastingly, but who also begin to rule the creation as servants of God already now, so that God's purpose with children in Genesis 1:28 is realized in them. "Out of the mouth of babes and sucklings thou hast perfected praise" (Matt. 21:16). This is why our children are a blessing, not a curse. This is the joy of the godly mother that swallows up all her sorrows, especially the sorrow of bearing sinful children. This makes all of the toil and sacrifice of believing parents worthwhile. They rear children who are "an heritage of the Lord," so that these children may praise God in time and eternity.

Already in Eve's case, the joy of motherhood had precedence over the sorrows. First, God promised her "the seed" which would bruise the devil's head: Jesus Christ and the elect multitude from Eve who are in Christ. Then, and only then, God spoke of the great sorrows of childbearing.

In light of this, it is not surprising that in history it has been the devil who has been the outstanding advocate of birth prevention in the church and, failing in that, of the murder of the infants of believers. It was he who moved the Pharaoh of Exodus 1 to enslave and afflict Israel, so that they would not multiply. When God frustrated this plan and blessed Israel with many children, it was he who attempted to murder the newly born male children. He knows that many children are a strength of the church, because of the covenant of God.

Even the fruitfulness of the marriage of believers belongs to the symbolism of marriage as a picture of the marriage of Christ and the church. Marriage is the mystery of Christ and the church. Christ begets many sons and daughters by His Word and Spirit. He has a large family, a multitude no man can number. To them, He is willing to devote His care. Christ even gave His life for them. Christ brings these children forth from and rears them by the church, His Bride. The union of Christ and the church is fruitful in many children of God. The church is the Mother of the saints by the power of the grace of Christ. So we sing in a version of Psalm 87:

> When the Lord shall count the nations,
> Sons and daughters He shall see,
> Born to endless life in Zion,
> And their joyful song shall be,
> "Blessed Zion, All our fountains are in thee,
> Blessed Zion, All our fountains are in thee."

So closely connected are the symbol, our marriages, and the reality, Christ's union with the church, that God uses the symbol to bring forth those who participate in the reality.

Therefore, Christian husbands and wives are still addressed by the Lord in the words of the prophet in Jeremiah 29:5, 6:

"Build ye houses, and dwell in them; and plant gardens, and eat the fruit of them; Take ye wives, and beget sons and daughters; and take wives for your sons, and give your daughters to husbands, that they may bear sons and daughters; that ye may be increased there, and not diminished."

The Calling of the Truly Liberated Woman

Kenneth Koole

The life which God has prescribed for covenant women in the church is not the way of the woman's liberation movement, but a life of child-bearing. In a sermon on I Timothy 2:11-15 Rev. Kenneth Koole points out God's command for women which is also their salvation. This sermon was delivered in Faith Protestant Reformed Church in Jenison, Michigan, of which Rev. Koole is pastor.

The Calling of the Truly Liberated Woman

Let the woman learn in silence with all subjection.
But I suffer not a woman to teach, nor to usurp authority over the man, but to be in silence.
For Adam was first formed, then Eve.
And Adam was not deceived, but the woman being deceived was in the transgression.
Notwithstanding she shall be saved in childbearing, if they continue in faith and charity and holiness with sobriety.

I Timothy 2:11-15

Our worship services are being advertised in the local paper. Perhaps you saw there the subject of this sermon. It was put in the form of a question — "What is the Place of the Christian, Believing Woman in the Church?" There is, as you know, great agitation today against what historically has been considered the Reformed and Scriptural place of the woman in the church.

In reaction to that agitation and in accordance with our text, I am inclined to answer the question in two phrases and to stop there. What's the place of the believing woman in the church? To be quiet and to bear children! It is as simple as that. You are dismissed.

Now, admittedly, that is a bit of a reactionary statement. It may be short and to the point, but it hardly does full justice to the place of the God-fearing woman in the church. According to the Scriptures this place, when the woman occupies it properly, is a place of beauty not only, but also one of power and of tremendous influence. This very congregation is testimony to that. If it were not for believing mothers who occupied their place and taught their children in the home, there would be no congregation here, or at least it would be quite different from what it presently is. Behind every great man, they say, stands his mother. So behind the church of Christ stand the mothers of Israel.

Today, of course, the hue and cry is for women to have a say in the government of the church, by which is meant their voting at congregational meetings, holding the offices, and thus determining the policies of the church by voice and vote. To that our church, our denomination, and a few others with it yet say "NO." And to that stand there is, as you know, a militant reaction. The charge is: You will not grant women their equal rights? You are against women.

It is not a matter, first of all, whether we are for or against women. There are some other considerations that shed light on whether we are for or against women. And the first consideration is, what saith the Scriptures? Are we for or against the Scriptures?

There is also another consideration that has bearing. And that is this, are we *for the church?* And that, you understand, the believing woman must ask, too. Are you, as believing women, for the church, your Lord's church? His church comes first. How can you be of greatest value to Christ's church? How can you best minister to this body as Christ calls every one of us as believers to minister?

The point of the text is that the woman ministers in a peculiar, unique way. She is saved by child-bearing. The church is saved through her child-bearing. It is exactly by what takes place in the home with the believing mothers that you have the building of the church. Thus the woman serves the church and Christ in a most powerful way.

Today women want to hold office. They are not happy in the home. They want to be out of the home. Outside the role of motherhood they will seek fulfillment. But the Word of God is that then they forsake the way of salvation. And to be a church that declares anything else, approving of the woman's lib movement, is not to be a friend of the gospel of Christ, but it is to be an enemy of the gospel of Christ. Those who promote that mentality will in the end pay a terrible price.

That church which, with the support of the believing women in her midst, is faithful in this declaration and calling will reap a rich harvest to be found in this life not only, but in the life to come. Why? Because it is the work of the mothers in the home that is an everlasting work. From a certain point of view, it is the only work that will ever endure. It is destined to outlast the work the man does in the work-a-day world and office. Mothers, for their encouragement, must keep this in mind.

Resisting Rebellion

We live in a day and age when the Scripture and its truth concerning the honorable, influential place of the woman is being assaulted.

The Calling of the Truly Liberated Woman

There are strident voices of dissatisfaction raised against what historically has been woman's lot in life both in society and in the church. That is not surprising. All the principles of Scripture are being assaulted. This one is no exception. Yet this assault is special in its nature. It is special because it takes us back to the very beginning. The devil, having once tempted the woman concerning her contentment with her place in the original Paradise, now tempts her once again with respect to her place in Christ's church and society and the home.

The hue and cry, as you know, is for liberation, meaning liberation from man, from male domination; liberation from the tyranny of men; and not simply that, but liberation from his headship and his rule altogether.

Women are laying claim to full and equal rights in all spheres of life. Supposedly the misery and the burdens and the secondary role and status that women have had to endure is all the fault of the men. And it is by means of rebellion and refusal to submit, or ever again to be subordinate, that woman will gain to herself equal status and rights, and achieve fulfillment and real happiness. So, they speak of this liberation.

Those who speak of this liberation, however, do not speak of it in terms of grace or of the salvation that is to be found in Christ Jesus. They will divorce these things. It is simply a liberation achieved by going their own willful, headstrong way.

We must understand that to speak of liberation and then to divorce it from the Word, from heart-changing grace, and from salvation is an exercise that is doomed to failure. It, in the end, is not a liberation at all. It is simply a continuation of woman's bondage to sin, and it is sure to increase their misery; misery of a new kind perhaps, but misery nonetheless.

The woman's lib movement, as you know, has kept a well-thumbed catalog of the abuses that the woman has suffered throughout the history of this world. They point to the abuses that women have experienced, to their pain, to their sorrow, to the burdens which they have simply been expected to suffer through in silence, meekly, while the male goes his carefree, recreational way.

They have catalogued the many ways in which women have been taken advantage of, treated often in degrading fashion. Often men have valued their horses more than they valued their wives. Their horses cost more.

Women remind you of the double standard that men have used in their treatment of women. These are not so hard to find. In the past it was lawful for a man to have one wife, two wives, three wives, or more, and then cheat on them all, and nary a word was to be said. But let one of those wives cheat on this same lecherous husband, and the law would come to bear. That woman was worthy of death. Or, if her husband killed her in outrage, it was justified. You regularly find that kind of mentality in man's history, this double standard.

There is the on-going abuse by a man who charms a woman off her feet, promises her the world, uses her, impregnates her, and then leaves her to her child-bearing and its burdens while he goes his merry way and charms another off her feet and carries on in the same fashion. And this is justice? Only a male would think it so.

That such has been all too common in man's treatment of the weaker vessel, we do not and cannot dispute. Men have taken advantage of women, and of their wives in particular, with horrible regularity.

So we come to the question: if this is how it so commonly has been in the world with the woman, then what is the solution? And when we ask what is the solution and remedy, we mean by that, what does God's Word say? What is God's way of deliverance from woman's sorrow with its burdens, and what is God's way for the woman to attain true happiness? That is the question. The answer we find in our text.

Let us understand that women and mothers will not find their relief by turning to the women's lib movement. It does not have the solution. And it does not because the women libbers do not understand the reason and the cause of woman's sorrows from its very beginning. And refusing to understand the real cause and origin, they can not give the remedy either.

The problem has been diagnosed by the experts in society. The problem has been diagnosed as the submission that has been forced upon the woman. It is her passive subordination to this state of affairs that has put her in this unhappy and intolerable situation. So they propose a rebellion against this spirit of quiet submission. It is time for the woman to rear back and to stand her ground and demand equal rights and to refuse to be used by men any longer. It means demanding equal say-so in all matters of life, church and home included.

You understand that is not the solution. That is not the biblical answer. The proposed solution is a lie. And because it is the lie, it is not liberation and freedom at all; it can tend only to a greater bondage and a deepening of the misery of mankind.

The apostle Paul, in our text, begins to give the solution, the way for woman to attain true freedom and happiness in exchange for her misery and despair, and to be a true blessing to the home and to Christ's church, which has to do with child-bearing.

In this connection it is important to understand what the problem is, what it is that has to be remedied, and what the cause of woman's whole predicament is. And that you find in verse 14. "And Adam was not deceived, but the woman being deceived was in the transgression."

Paul's point here is that the first sin was Eve's sin. Sin originated with Eve's eating of the fruit. It was not Adam who was first deceived. Eve was first deceived by the Deceiver. She ate. She gave to her husband, enticed him, and then together they fell.

Now it is not Paul's point nor intention to lay upon woman all the blame, as though Adam is without fault in the whole matter. Adam, too, had guilt. Adam also is to blame for the fall. When he ate, he ate as the head of the human race, and he did that fully aware that what he was doing was forbidden. His mouth watered for the forbidden fruit. And the consequence, as you know, was death with all of its attendant miseries. The man also bears this responsibility from the beginning.

Rather, Paul's point is this, that as woman considers her lot in life, her sorrows and her burdens, then she must not simply fault man and thus refuse to own up to her own responsibility and the part she had to play in bringing her distress upon herself. How easy to reason, "It was all Adam's fault. After all, he was the head. Man still runs the show. And so the mess we are in is to be laid entirely at his feet." There is then this bitterness over against the man; he is to blame; and one resents his maleness. And woman concludes, "My predicament is all man's fault."

That, however, is not how it is. The first sin was not Adam's, it was Eve's. Woman had a part to play, a large part, in bringing upon herself the very burdens and the sorrows that she resents. And even the sufferings men experience come as a consequence of her choice in the garden.

The question that confronts us then is: what was this first sin? As we already suggested, it had to do with this rebellion; Eve rebelling at the very beginning against her calling to be submissive, that is, to be content to be a help fit for the man, quietly to learn what the will of her husband was, and then to act accordingly. To put it simply, she decided she would determine for herself what was right and what was wrong. She would act independently and consult Adam not at all. Of course not; she feared what Adam might say. Adam might well have said, "Don't eat of it. That is forbidden."

We ourselves know that, do we not? When we see something that plain as day is sin, but we want it, we do not first consult someone else by asking, "What do you advise?" do we? Of course not. We fear what they may say, namely, "Don't do it." And so they would interfere with our pleasure. Young people are tempted to go to the theater? Well, do not talk to your parents about this. They will probably forbid it and so interfere with your pleasure. So, just strike out on your own. How well we know that nature. It is our own.

So with Eve towards Adam at the very beginning. Weary of subordination she would act upon her own, independently, and be her own lord. So she ate and she fell. And then came the avalanche of consequences.

If the first sin was the woman's refusal to submit herself to male headship, and this was the origin of woman's sorrows and burdens, to say nothing of society's miseries, then how can we propose this as the *solution?* This is precisely Paul's point.

In verses 11 and 12 he has forbidden women to teach or to usurp authority over the man. And as the whole epistle makes plain, he is dealing with the woman's place in the church. There they were to be silent. For them even to attempt to teach (speak with authority) was itself a usurping of authority, and hence sin. So much for women elders, preachers, and even deacons. Such are positions of teaching authority.

And now it is in this connection that Paul makes reference to woman's first transgression, which was obviously one of usurping authority. Instead of consulting Adam, Eve proceeds on her own, not seeking direction from him at all. Such is the origin of woman's sorrows and travails. She despised the way of submission, she wearied of recognizing man's headship. And now this is to be the remedy — woman's acting the very same way? That is how it all began. And now this is how it is all to be resolved — by doing it all over again? And thus the problems will disappear?

Paul's point is: of course not. That is sheer folly. All it is going to do is intensify the problems that already stand between man and woman. All such behavior will do is to bring more warfare and conflict, and with it, bitter consequences. Nothing else.

Further, let us understand that Paul's point is that this calling to submit is nothing less than a creation ordinance. That is verse 13: "For Adam was first formed, then Eve." In other words, this whole business of subordination and submission was not man's grand idea, something that man simply decided to impose upon woman because of his superior strength. No, this was God's will from the beginning. God made man first because he was to be the head, and He made woman from man's rib, given to man to assist him in his calling. God ordained this order. And these two by occupying their respective places would then function as one, as head and body.

So when one rebels against this order, one is not rebelling simply against sinful man or an insensitive husband. Rather, one is rebelling against the Creator Himself. This being the case, despising man's headship can not be the solution for the woman. That must lie in another direction.

The woman must be warned. She is not to listen to Satan's siren song again. He came at the very dawn of history with this temptation to be insubordinate. "Yea, hath God said...?" Is that really God's word? And you are satisfied with that? You are going to live by God's word when He denies you this obvious pleasure? You are not going to determine for yourself your place in creation and in society, home, and church? What the preacher says from the pulpit — you are going to be content with that? Or with what your husband says? You are just going to accept that? You have a mind; you have intelligence; make some decisions on your own. That is the devil's approach. These were his first words. And the consequences came flooding in as a result. And so the tempter continues using the same approach. "Do not listen to

God's Word; do not look to your husband for leadership; determine your life for yourself. And that will be your liberation and your freedom."

The believing woman must learn from that sin, that first transgression made at the beginning. She must not imitate Eve in this action, because in the end that is not liberation or true freedom, but instead the bringer of great grief. Rather the mothers of Israel must listen to God's Word. Certainly the One who made woman knows better than any what it is that will give her happiness and in the end even fulfillment in this life and in the life to come.

Bearing Children

The text ties together the woman's happiness and fulfillment with the burden of child-bearing. "Notwithstanding, she shall be saved by child-bearing." That means, though there may be these sorrows and these pains of motherhood, and though the woman introduced them into the world by her folly in the beginning, yet God in His mercy is not going to abandon the woman to her curse and to all of her burdens, but He is going to make a way out, a way of deliverance. And this has to do with child-bearing. "She shall be saved in child-bearing" (vs. 15).

Now, that word *'saved'* does not have to do here, first of all, with the forgiveness of sins, as though in some way bearing children is a penance and by enduring the pain of child-bearing that the woman makes payment for her original sin. This cannot be. What shall be said then of the woman who has the barren womb and never experiences the pangs of child-birth? Is she excluded from the kingdom and salvation? That cannot be.

It says here, not "because of child-bearing," or "on the basis of child-bearing," but "through child-bearing." This is the God-ordained way of salvation. This has to do with the way out.

This is important in our consideration. It means: child-bearing brings salvation and deliverance from the sorrows and miseries that have resulted from the fall.

From a certain point of view that sounds strange, that for the woman child-bearing is the way of deliverance from her sorrows, because, as so many of you know full well, it is exactly in bearing children that one experiences so much pain and discomfort. And each child adds to the burden of motherhood. And this is to be the way out?

Nonetheless, the Lord God in His wisdom determined that in this way of pain and sorrow that women, the daughters of Eve, would triumph over pain and misery.

This can be seen in the instance of Eve herself. For her, childbearing, for all of its attendant griefs and pains, was the only way of salvation and deliverance. This was what gave her hope. Imagine if following the fall the same Lord God who had said to our first parents "Be fruitful and multiply" had said to Eve, "Because of your sin I am going to shut your womb. You have forfeited the right to bring forth children. You shall die when very old, but childless! That is My judgment on you." Or, "I may give you a few children, but your daughters, everyone of them, will be barren." Whence then salvation? Whence the seed of the woman? Whence then Christ?

God came with a promise — the mother promise — in which was wrapped salvation. He spoke of the seed of the woman, through which seed He would give the victory over the seed of the serpent, crushing its head. He was speaking, of course, ultimately of the victory over death's poisonous sting and the evil world. But that is only because of the seed of the woman and its birth.

Now we know, of course, that the heart of the seed of the woman is Christ Himself, but what we must understand is that when mention is made of the seed of the woman and the victory which the church attains through that seed, God is not speaking only of Christ. Rather He is referring to all the elect children, to the whole church that would be born, to all the Abels, Seths, Isaacs, and Jacobs.

All of Eve's believing children have been active participants in the great battle of the ages, the battle of faith. All of them have withstood Satan and his designs. By God they have been used to cause Satan and his cause to suffer setbacks, striking setbacks, and the alteration of his designs. God has used many of Eve's children to snatch victory from the jaws of apparent defeat. Some of the outstanding examples would be Noah, Moses, David, Rahab, Sarah, and Ruth. They too have contributed to the victory of the church.

And the point is that this includes our own children whom we by the grace of God are privileged to bring forth.

Note, and note well, that the text tells us that the Lord God has determined to save through child-bearing. Today, that has completely lost its appeal, also in the church. Surely, our gifted women can not be tied down with child-bearing. They must be out liberating the world! There are greater things for the woman to accomplish for the church than mere child-bearing!

Mothers and fathers of Israel, do we see that? Do we understand that — that the victory of the church and that the hope of the church (and of God's world itself) in the end is not determined by the occupation the man has, whether he is a construction worker, whether he is busy in agriculture, whether he is an accountant, or if he works in the factory, or what have you?

It does not have to do with those so-called glamourous careers that the men occupy and cause women's heads to spin, the big-money jobs. Jobs are a necessary "evil" if the family is to have the where-with-all to live. But do you not see, that is not how the church is gathered. That is not how the church of Christ gains the victory. That is not how the power of Satan and of hell is crushed and given stunning defeat.

Satan and all the fiends of hell could care less if you and I were to earn ten times more than we do now. In fact if it were up to him, we would probably all be filthy rich. That is no threat to his kingdom and his designs.

Do we understand what it is that shakes Satan's kingdom to its very foundation and strikes dread into his fiendish heart? I will tell you. It is the cry of birth-pangs coming from the mouth of a God-fearing mother; it is the wail of a child that has been born in a believing home. That is what strikes fear and dread into the heart of the Evil One, because that means that his design is not succeeding. The church is not being choked out, but the church is living and growing, and by faith in the covenant promise, still bringing forth.

There are many cries and groans of pain made by mankind that cause Satan delight. But there is no sound more grating to the ears of Satan than the groans of mothers bringing forth the true Israel. In that cry he does not gloat. Who knows what these little ones will grow up to be and how they will withstand his kingdom!

It is in them that there is the power of life. It is in them that is the power of faith to withstand his temptations and to expose his falsehoods. It is from them that you will find those who will serve as a Moses

The Calling of the Truly Liberated Woman

or an Elijah or as a Luther, a Calvin, a Ruth, a Deborah, or a Sarah and all the rest. There is a power of Christ in them.

In the Old Testament we know well that child-bearing prepared the way of Christ. In the way of child-bearing He came.

You understand, so it is in the New Testament, this present age. Christ shall come again. But He can come and He will come only when the last elect child has been born so that He might have the last one for whom He shed His blood. And when the last elect comes forth and expresses faith, then comes the end of all things and the return of the King.

And this is why the Scriptures focus our attention not upon the big business and the glamorous career. About such things the Scriptures could care less. Rather Scripture directs us to the beauty of the God-fearing home. Why? Because what is going to endure is not the new house we have put up, nor what has been accomplished at the office or in the business world; but what is going to stand forever and what is going to defeat Satan in the end are those who as little ones have learned the name of Christ and then later make confession concerning His great name and truth.

It is in the covenant home that you have those who are being trained as the instruments of a spiritual warfare. Satan knows full well that it is from the Christian, God-fearing home that there will come well-trained believers whose faith he cannot withstand and who will acquaint others with Christ as well. And keep in mind that the mother is the heart of the home, her love, her labor.

Do you think it makes Satan sad to see covenant homes empty, the mothers out in the work-a-day world? Do you think this does not play right into his hands? I tell you of a truth there are any number who can replace us males in whatever job we hold down. But you try to replace the mother in the home, in what she is doing. There is no replacement.

You understand, the mother is vital. The mothers in Israel are involved in a great work. Walter Chantry states it well when he writes: "Talents are to be developed; virtues must be instilled: faults are to be patiently corrected; [and we might add, sins rooted out—KK]. She (the mother) is building men and women for God. Results may not be visible until she has labored fifteen to twenty years. Even when her task ends, the true measure of her work awaits the full maturity of her children." Indeed, the fullness of her work will be revealed in eternity.

Men may work with wood; they may work with stone; they may be artists and craftsmen. What of that is going to stand when Christ comes again? It is all going to be removed. There is one great work that will not be removed, but shall endure, and that is the life of the child who has been formed and molded by believing hands. This is the work which shall endure with its fruits.

Persevering in Faithfulness

God-fearing mothers are involved in a great work. They need much encouragement. They also need many virtues and spiritual gifts. That is why Paul speaks of their continuing in faith and charity and holiness with sobriety. The point is, just having children is not the whole of obedience to what the apostle is prescribing here. Rather it is bearing children and then persevering in the work. That is what is necessary. Great spiritual virtues will be needed in the work. And it is only by patient persistence in displaying these virtues that the mother's labor will bear full spiritual fruit in her children's lives.

Faith comes into play. Faith is needed to encourage a woman in her work. She must trust that the Lord Who requires this of her knows best. And as she believes and looks to the Good Shepherd, she teaches the lambs also to look to the same Shepherd, teaching them to trust His power and the wisdom of His Word.

Love, of course, has to do with sacrifice, and seeking the well-being of another. There is certainly much self-sacrifice required in the demanding labor of motherhood. Love is what will give her incentive to persevere in her labor for her family. And this labor of love is not without its rewards. Like the love of Christ for us, it will bear its peaceable fruit, the fruit of godliness and daily conversion.

Paul also mentions holiness. Holiness has to do with purity. And so Paul also speaks of sobriety, or more literally, discernment. In the end it falls upon the mother to teach her children right from wrong, and good over against evil. She teaches her children what things are pure and holy and hence to be desired, and what is evil, what displeases God, and must therefore be rejected. She needs great spiritual discernment to do this. All these things the woman needs for her own salvation and these are the virtues she seeks to convey to her children as well.

The woman was instrumental in bringing sorrows and miseries upon mankind. How will she participate in undoing that? How but by child-bearing, bringing forth the Christ, bringing forth the church, and those who gather the church. It is the great work that itself shall endure. It is a work in which we must all be busy. We have been given children, but how long shall we keep these children? How diligent should we not be in their instruction in the time allotted!

Can you imagine that a parent will ever regret one moment that has been spent with one's child, instructing that child in the ways of the Lord? Time marches on, and as time marches on we must continue to instruct, occupying our place. This is true of the woman especially, silent in the church, but teaching in the home. And the work of her hands in her home 'ministry' will bear much fruit for herself, for her family, and for the church itself, unto all eternity. This is redemption in the full sense of the word.

Letter to Timothy

Herman C. Hanko

When the question of the right of women to hold the office of deacon in the church first came up in the Christian Reformed Church in the late seventies, it was predicted that this was but the stepping stone to the opening of all offices in the church to women. The question of deaconesses received careful scrutiny on the basis of Scripture in a series of articles which appeared in the *Standard Bearer* in December, 1978, and January, 1979. Proceeding from the premise that the office of deacons is also an *authoritative* office in the church, these articles show that also women deacons are forbidden by Scripture. Prof. Herman Hanko is professor of New Testament and historical theology in the Protestant Reformed Seminary in Grand Rapids, Michigan.

> Note of explanation:
> These articles were written as "Letters to Timothy" in Prof. Hanko's rubric in the *Standard Bearer*. We leave this format unchanged in our reprinting here.

December 15, 1978

Dear Timothy,

In our discussion of the offices in the church of Christ, we must now turn to the office of deacon.

You reminded me in your last letter of the fact that, among many different denominations, it is becoming customary practice to ordain women in office; and you mentioned specifically the recent decisions of the Christian Reformed Church which granted the right to women to serve in the office of deacon. You asked me if I would make some comments about this in connection with these letters on the offices.

I do not intend to write concerning the whole question of women elders and women ministers; but it would be worth our while to discuss this matter of women deacons in the light of recent Christian Reformed Synodical decisions.

One of the texts quoted in support of the contention that women may function in the office of deacon is Romans 16:1, 2: "I commend unto you Phebe our sister, which is a servant of the church which is at Cenchrea: That ye receive her in the Lord, as becometh saints, and that ye assist her in whatsoever business she hath need of you: for she hath been a succourer of many, and of myself also." The reason why this passage is quoted in support of women deacons is because the word "servant" in the phrase, "a servant of the church which is at Cenchrea" can correctly be translated "deaconess." It is the same word, though in the feminine, which in other parts of Scripture is translated "deacon." The conclusion is therefore made that Phebe was a deaconess in the church at Cenchrea and that this had the apostle's sanction. Because the apostle Paul was a means whereby God gave us the Scriptures, his word is to be considered regulative for us also in this respect.

We ought to look at this whole matter a bit because, although many other texts are quoted and discussed in connection with this controversy, this is in a sense the key passage, for it is the only one where there is any *positive* statement which seems to allow for deaconesses.

The Scriptures do not tell us a great deal about Phebe. In fact, all the information we have of her is found in this passage.

The city of Cenchrea of which she was a resident was located just a little to the south and east of Corinth in the southern part of the Greek peninsula which was known as Achaia. The church in Cenchrea was probably established on Paul's second missionary journey during the time of his labor in Corinth. Paul often made one city the center of his labors, and the gospel went forth from that center to all the surrounding area (confer Acts 19:10).

Phebe may have been a woman of some means who was traveling to Rome on business for he tells the Roman church to "assist her in whatsoever business she hath need of you."

If it is true that Paul's letter to the Romans was written from Corinth (and this is likely), then it may be that he sent his epistle to the Romans by her hand. That would explain the commendation he gives her in these two verses of Romans 16. At any rate, this has been the traditional opinion of the church; and so we read at the end of the epistle: "Written to the Romans from Corinthus, and sent by Phebe servant of the church at Cenchrea."

The Lord had saved her and she occupied an important place in the church at Cenchrea — whatever now that place may have been.

Paul himself stopped in Cenchrea after he had finished his work in Corinth and prior to going to Jerusalem. There he had shaved his head in fulfillment of a vow he had made to God.

This is about all that is known of Phebe.

The question is: was she a deaconess?

As far as the word itself is concerned, it is true as some have argued that the word translated "servant" in Romans 16:1 can just as well be translated "deaconess." We readily grant this. It is striking, however, that the translators of the King James Version of the Bible did not do this; and we may well ask: why?

Other than in this passage, there are only two places in the whole New Testament Scriptures where this word actually refers to the office of deacon. It might be well to take a look at these passages a moment, for they have some bearing on the matter. The first place is I Timothy

3:8-13 which reads: "Likewise must the deacons be grave, not double-tongued, not given to much wine, not greedy of filthy lucre; holding the mystery of the faith in a pure conscience. And let these also first be proved; then let them use the office of a deacon, being found blameless. Even so must their wives be grave, not slanderers, sober, faithful in all things. Let the deacons be the husbands of one wife, ruling their children and their own houses well. For they that have used the office of a deacon well purchase to themselves a good degree, and great boldness in the faith which is in Christ Jesus."

The reason why I have quoted this passage is not only that it is one of the two places where the word for "deacon" appears in reference to the office, but also because this passage too has been quoted to prove the existence of deaconesses in the apostolic church. The argument is based on verse 11. The King James Version reads: "Even so must their wives be grave, not slanderers, sober, faithful in all things." The word translated "wives" can also be translated "women"; and the word "their," referring to the deacons themselves, is not found in the Greek — which is why it appears in the King James Version in italics. There are, therefore, different translations of this. Philips translates this verse: "Their wives should share their serious outlook" and contains the same idea as the King James Version. The New English Bible does the same: "Their wives, equally, must be women of high principle." The New International Version does the same. But the Revised Standard Bible does not: "The women likewise must be serious."

So there are different translations and interpretations of this passage. Hendrickson says the passages refer to deacons' helpers. Lenski claims the passage refers to deaconesses. And others insist that the reference is to deacons' wives. We agree with this latter. Rev. George Lubbers writes in the *Standard Bearer* (Vol. 38, p. 203):

> The first interpretation holds that Paul here speaks of the requisites for women to be elected to the *office* of deaconess. The reasons assigned by these is that the term "likewise" in verse 11, must, just as in verse 8, refer to a transition to a new class of office....
>
> The second interpretation holds that Paul here speaks of the "wives" of deacons. Attention is called to the fact that Paul does not really begin to speak of a new and different class of officebearers — deaconesses, but that he must refer to the wives of deacons since he inserts this instruction in the midst of his instruction concerning the necessary qualifications of the

deacons who will be called to the office. Besides, it is noticed that Paul does not here speak of "deaconesses" but that he simply speaks of "women," while there are passages where Paul, referring to women set aside to the special ministry in the church, denominates these with the name "deaconesses" or "servant."

We are of the opinion that the latter interpretation is the correct one.

We might add to the above that the very same word is used in the following verse where emphatically Paul writes: "Let the deacons be the husbands of one wife." If Paul were, in verse 11, referring to the special office of deaconess, it would have been very easy for him to use the word for deaconess here and not a word which in the immediately following verse must be translated wife.

So this passage refers to the qualifications of the office of deacon and clearly teaches that all these qualifications belong to deacons who are men.

The second passage where the word "deacon" refers to the special office in the church is in Philippians 1:1: "Paul and Timotheus, the servants of Jesus Christ, to all the saints in Christ Jesus which are at Philippi, with the bishops and deacons."

Here the reference is to the special office of the diaconate because "deacons" are mentioned in one breath with "bishops" — another name for elders which could better be translated "overseers."

These then are the only two places where the word clearly refers to the special office.

But there are innumerable places where the word cannot possibly refer to the special office of deacon. There are so many that we can scarcely choose between them. But two passages will suffice. In John 20:26 Jesus says: "If any man serve me, let him follow me; and where I am, there shall also my servant be: if any man serve me, him will my Father honor." In this passage, the word translated "servant" is the same word which can be translated "deacon." But it is clear from this passage that it cannot have a reference to the special office of deacon, for Jesus is talking about all His people who serve Him.

In Matthew 23:11 we read: "But he that is greatest among you shall be your servant." Here too the reference obviously cannot be to the special office of deacon even though the word "servant" is the same as that translated deacon in I Timothy 3.

What we have proved is that this word, while it can be translated "deacon," nevertheless need not be. And this is because its general meaning is taken from a verb which means "to minister to the needs of another."

Now, having proceeded this far in the argument we shall also have to show that the word as used in Romans 16:1 cannot be correctly translated as "deaconess."

This can easily be proved.

It must be remembered first of all that which I said to you in an earlier article concerning the work of the offices in the church in general. You remember that I stressed the fact that the three offices had this in common that they all brought the Word of God to God's people. They all do this in keeping with the particular nature of their office, but nevertheless, they are all servants of the Word. They all speak in Christ's name. They all are ministers of Christ's Word. They all have no authority outside that authoritative Word. The ministers speak that Word as prophets who bring the Word through the preaching. The elders speak that Word as king and rule by that Word in the congregation. The deacons bring that Word as it speaks of the mercy of Christ to His afflicted people. But they bring the Word. To say anything else is to misunderstand badly the office. This is why also our Form for Ordination defines the duty of the deacons to be to bring to the poor "comforting words from Scripture."

This whole question must be examined a bit more in detail in connection with the subject of deaconesses. But we shall have to wait with this for a future letter.

Fraternally in Christ,
H. Hanko

January 1, 1979

Dear Timothy,

In our last letter we had turned to a discussion of the work of deacons. I answered in part your questions concerning the recent decision of the Christian Reformed Church to allow women into the office of deacons provided that they were not considered as elders and given the same authority as elders. But I did not finish this question: we talked about the use of the term "deacon" and the term "deaconess" in Scripture and found that the argument of the Christian Reformed Church was fallacious on this point. But there is another aspect to this question which we must now discuss.

The whole argument of the decision of the Christian Reformed Church quite obviously hinges on the erroneous idea that deacons do not exercise authority within the church. That this is the argument (although it is not explicitly stated) is evident from the fact that the decision refuses to allow women to serve as elders or ministers, and refuses to allow a congregation to install deaconesses if these women should in any way share in the work of elders or possess in some way the authority which elders possess.

This position is by no means the position of all within the Christian Reformed Church. There are those who take the position that women may function in all these offices; and they insist that the churches grievously err when they deny these offices to women. But there are others (and they prevailed at Synod) who believe that women may not serve as elders and ministers but may serve as deacons, because there is no authority exercised in the office of deacon.

To put it a little differently: there are passages in the Scriptures which speak of women exercising authority in the church. But there are differences of interpretation concerning these passages. The two clearest passages are I Corinthians 14:34, 35 and I Timothy 2:11, 12. Those who do not believe that women ought to be elders and ministers appeal to these passages as decisive. Those who do maintain that women may also function in the church as elders and ministers consider these passages to be stipulations which apply to Paul's day, but that they have no normative force for the church of today.

So there are three positions: 1) Those who maintain that women may not be officebearers at all; 2) Those who maintain that women may be deaconesses but not ministers and elders; 3) Those who maintain that women may serve in any office.

We are primarily concerned now with the second group. And we are concerned with that group because their position is, apparently, that the office of deacon is an office without authority. So we have to show two things. We have to show first of all that the two passages to which we referred above specifically deny women authority in the church; and we have to show that the office of deacon is also an office of authority. If these two things can be shown, then we must conclude that the Scriptures forbid women officebearers.

That the two passages to which we referred earlier deny women a position of authority in the church is admitted by almost every one. So clear is this that even those who insist that women are permitted to hold office do not question the interpretation of the passages so much; they rather simply relegate these passages to the dust pile of outmoded practices. They were relevant for Paul's day when women were considered inferior; but they are no longer of interest or concern to us now that we have learned that women and men are on a plane of equality.

The two passages read: "Let your women keep silence in the churches: for it is not permitted unto them to speak; but they are commanded to be under obedience, as also saith the law. And if they will learn any thing, let them ask their husbands at home: for it is a shame for women to speak in the church" (I Cor. 14:34, 35). "Let the women learn in silence with all subjection. But I suffer not a woman to teach, nor to usurp authority over the man, but to be in silence" (I Tim. 2:11, 12).

These texts are clear. There are a couple of points which we can briefly notice. 1) They both speak of the church, and this is usually agreed upon by all commentators. The passage in Corinthians clearly speaks of the church, for it is mentioned in so many words: "Let your women keep silence in the churches ... for it is a shame for women to speak in the church." This is also true of the passage in Timothy, however. The whole chapter deals with practices in the church. In the first verses already Paul is talking about prayers which ought to be uttered in the church services which Timothy as a minister of the gospel is called to lead. Never has the church applied this passage to life in general. Paul suffers not a woman to teach; but no one, to my knowledge, has ever said that a woman may not teach her children in the home; that a woman may not teach in Christian schools; that a woman may not teach in Sunday School, provided that the Sunday School is kept separate from the institutional life of the church. 2) They both enjoin women to silence. That is, while both enjoin upon women submission to authority, both also expressly state that women must be silent. They may not teach. And, their subjection to authority within the church is expressly described as silence in the official and institutional life of the church. 3) Paul states in Corinthians that this is not merely a rule which he thinks appropriate for the circumstances in which the churches of his day find themselves, but he specifically states that this is a matter of the law: "as also saith the law." The whole normative force of the law of God is at stake here.

This teaches therefore, without doubt, that women may occupy no position of authority within the church — especially not a position of authority in which they *speak*. And so the question is: is this true of the office of deacons? Everyone recognizes that it is true of the office of elders and of the office of ministers. But is it also true of the office of deacons? That is the question which needs yet to be answered.

There are several reasons why we must take the position that also deacons exercise authority in the church and are called to speak the Word of God. We shall take the time to enumerate these reasons and discuss them briefly.

1) There are two places where the Scriptures speak of the qualifications of deacons, and both places mention qualifications which refer to a special office of authority and bringing the Word. The first such passage is Acts 6:1-7 where we have the record of the institution of the office. The part of that passage which is of immediate interest to us is verse 3: "Wherefore, brethren, look ye out among you seven men of honest report, full of the Holy Ghost and wisdom, whom we may appoint over this business." Now it ought to be clear to anyone that if these men were entrusted with no other work than to provide sufficient food for the Grecian widows who were neglected in the daily ministrations, they would not have to be men who were full of the Holy Spirit and wisdom. It takes neither the Holy Spirit nor wisdom to see to it that certain widows have enough to eat. These qualifications speak clearly

of the fact that more was required of them. They were to have a work which they could perform only if they were full of the Holy Spirit and of wisdom. It is interesting to note, perhaps in passing, that at least two of these deacons also were evangelists who preached the gospel. Stephen and Philip both preached. And while this office of evangelist was unique in a certain sense, nevertheless, the early church apparently did not think it strange that two deacons should preach. If I were arguing for women elders and ministers, I would certainly appeal to this passage. I would argue: if the Scriptures permit women deacons, then we have no reason to forbid the offices of elders and ministers to women because it is clear from Acts that the two New Testament deacons also preached.

The same is true of the passage in I Timothy 3 where Paul specifically speaks of the qualifications of deacons. Among other things he mentions: "grave, not doubletongued," "holding the mystery of the faith in pure conscience," "ruling their children and their own houses well." Now, again, if the work of deacons is only to distribute money, why are these qualifications listed which have nothing to do with this work? Why must a deacon be grave and not doubletongued if he does not "speak" in the church anyway? Why must a deacon hold the mystery of the faith in a pure conscience if he is not to bring the Word of God to those in need? Why must a deacon show that he knows how to rule his children and his own house if he is not going to exercise authority in the church anyway? No, we must conclude that the office of deacon also involves speaking authoritatively the Word of God.

These passages of Scripture are decisive. If women are to keep silence in the church and not usurp authority over the man, then it surely follows that they cannot function in the office of deacon.

But there is more.

2) That deacons speak the Word of God authoritatively also follows from the very nature of the office. It is a fundamental principle of all Reformed church polity that Christ and Christ alone is the Officebearer in His church. This is expressly taught in many places, but Peter says this in so many words in I Peter 2:25: "For ye were as sheep going astray; but are now returned unto the Shepherd and Bishop of your souls." That Christ is the only Officebearer in His church means

simply that all the care of the church is exercised by Christ. He alone provides for all the needs of His people. He alone, as the good Shepherd, feeds and nourishes them. He alone saves and redeems them. He alone exercises all authority over them. And He does this in such a way that He is their Prophet and Priest and King. He feeds them with His Word. He rules over them and disciplines them. He cares for all their needs. He makes their griefs and sorrows, their sicknesses and poverty, their trouble and distress the object of His sympathetic and merciful care.

But this care of Christ is exercised over all His sheep through the offices which He has ordained in the church, for He is in heaven and we are on earth. We shall someday be in heaven, and then we shall have no further need of ministers, elders, and deacons for we shall be with Christ. But while we are on earth, we have this need. Christ provides it.

But the authority which He exercises through the offices is exercised through all the offices. There are not two offices which are authoritative and one which is not. This is absurd. If one is not, then it is simply not an office in the church. But all three are offices, instituted by Christ, through which Christ comes to us in all our need.

There are a few more reasons yet why we must consider the office of deacon authoritative; but we shall have to defer discussion of them till our next exchange of correspondence.

Fraternally in Christ,
H. Hanko

Letter to Timothy

January 15, 1979

Dear Timothy,

You will recall, if I may for a moment review our discussion, that we were talking about this whole question of whether the Scriptures permit women to hold the office of deacon. In an earlier letter we showed that the Scriptures nowhere speak of deaconesses. Because this was somewhat of an argument from silence, we went on to show that the Scriptures expressly forbid women to hold office in the church. We briefly examined two key passages, I Corinthians 14:34, 35, and I Timothy 2:11, 12, to show that women are enjoined by Scripture to keep silence in the church. But then, in order to answer the argument that this includes deaconesses, we began a discussion of the nature of the office of deacon to show that it is true of this office as well as of the offices of elder and minister that deacons exercise authority in the church and that they also are called to bring the Word of God. We argued, first of all, that this was true on the basis of the two passages where the office of deacon is spoken of in Scripture: Acts 6:1-7 and I Timothy 3:8-13. And we argued secondly, from the nature of the office itself. Christ is the only Officebearer in His church who provides for all the needs of His people. He does this through the special offices in the church because through these special offices He exercises authority over His people; but this authority is always the authority of His Word.

We must pursue this whole question a bit further.

When in the last letter I wrote to you that the office of deacon is an office in which deacons both exercise authority and bring the Word of God, I did not mean to say that these are two distinct functions of the office. You must not conclude from these remarks that the calling of deacons to bring God's Word to His people is distinct from the calling to exercise authority over God's people. This surely is not the case.

While it is true that the authority which any officebearer possesses in the church is an authority by virtue of his office to which Christ has called him, nevertheless, this authority is always and only the authority of the Word of Christ which the officebearer brings. Only Christ's Word ever has authority within the church. And the officebearers exercise authority only when they come with the Word of Christ.

So this leads us to the third remark we must make in connection with the right of men only to hold the office of deacon. It is not proper to distinguish between the office of deacon on the one hand and the offices of minister and elder on the other hand on the implicit or explicit grounds that deacons do not exercise authority, and that, therefore, as long as women remain deacons only, they may hold this office for they are not in violation of the Scriptural injunctions found in I Corinthians 14:34, 35 and I Timothy 2:11, 12. Or, to put it a little differently, if women are given the right to hold the office of deacon, they are given the right to "speak in the church," a right which Scripture expressly forbids.

And this brings us to the fourth point which needs to be made.

It has always been maintained in Reformed church polity that there is what can only be called a certain overlapping of the offices. While it certainly is true that each officebearer is called by Christ to bring the Word of Christ according to the nature of his own office whether minister, elder, or deacon, it is also true that because the authority of each office is the authority of the Word of Christ, these offices necessarily overlap somewhat in the actual life of the church. There are many instances of that. For one thing, even our Church Order provides for some such overlapping. In Article 16 the work of discipline is assigned to both ministers and elders: "The office of the ministry is to continue in prayer ... and, finally, with the elders, to exercise church discipline and to see to it that everything is done decently and in good order." More particularly, however, Article 37 reads: "Whenever the number of elders is small, the deacons may be added to the consistory by local regulation; this shall invariably be the rule where the number is less than three." Concerning this matter VanDellen and Monsma have some interesting remarks to make in their *Church Order Commentary*. They write:

First of all then, the three offices of the N.T. Church are derived from Christ's threefold office and correspond to these .... Each office has its distinct task, though the offices are more or less inter-related and they have their unity in Christ.

Whenever necessary these three types of officebearers may work together in governing the Churches and in caring for the poor. Elders then act as assistant Deacons and Deacons as assistant Elders. Thus it must be done in very small congregations, numbering less than three Elders.

This special arrangement of full cooperation of all the offices is altogether permissible in view of the essential unity of the office in Christ....

From the foregoing it will be clear that when the Deacons are part of the

Consistory they should be considered to be full-fledged Consistory members. They have a voice and vote in all matters which pertain to the government of the Church, even as the Elders under these circumstances have a voice and vote in all matters regarding the Church's work of mercy. To deny the Deacons a right to vote in cases of discipline, for instance, would be contrary to the Church Order and the duties which have been imposed on them by local arrangement (p. 166).

The question might be asked: But is this also true in those congregations where the elders and deacons meet separately? The answer is that even where elders and deacons meet separately, they nevertheless meet together in matters which pertain to the congregation as a whole, among which matters are matters which also concern the government of the church. VanDellen and Monsma quote Jansen on what matters ought to be treated by general meetings where both elders and deacons are present. These include: 1) All matters pertaining to the election of office-bearers: nominations; final decision whether or not one chosen shall be called; consideration of objections registered; releasing one from his call to office, etc. 2) The issuing and receiving of certificates of ministers arriving or departing. 3) Provisional consideration of and decision regarding emeritation. 4) Mutual censure. 5) Church visitation. 6) Administration of finances. 7) The general administration of benevolence matters. 8) General business administration of the material interests of the church. 9) Consideration of general correspondence.

Now it is clear from all this that even in those congregations where elders and deacons meet separately for their own unique work, there are many matters which must be dealt with by both elders and deacons. These matters involve the rule of the church. If women, therefore, are permitted to hold the office of deacon, they will also, in the nature of the case, be permitted a voice in certain aspects of the rule of the church. And then they will be in direct violation of the Scriptures.

This fact extends far beyond even what we have discussed above. If women are voted in as deacons there is nothing at all to prevent them from also leading worship services in the congregation in those places where deacons are added to the consistory. And so we could go on.

The whole point is that the principle of Article 84 of the Church Order is a Scriptural principle. Article 84 reads: "No church shall in any way lord it over other churches, no minister over other ministers, no elder or deacon over other elders or deacons." Positively stated, this article teaches that all the offices are on a plane of equality. And they are equal because they are all representatives of Christ through whom Christ is pleased to rule over His church.

There is still one other matter which we might mention in this connection.

It sometimes appears that those who argue in favor of women in office do so on the grounds that by excluding women from office, women are pushed into a position of inferiority in the church of Christ. The argument goes something like this. To hold an office is to hold a position of authority over others. Those who hold such positions of authority are, by virtue of that fact, placed in a superior position. Those who are excluded from such positions of authority are placed in positions of submission to authority, and are relegated to inferior positions in the church.

This is a false argument and is based on a serious misconception of the whole office. The Scriptures are very clear on the point that those who hold positions of authority within the church do not occupy superior positions over other so that they can, by virtue of their office, relegate others to a lower status. Quite the opposite is true. This is clear, for example, from the Lord's teachings in John 13:12-17. At the time of the last celebration of the Passover Feast with His disciples, Jesus had taken the opportunity to wash His disciples' feet. After finishing and after answering the objections of Peter, the Lord said: "Know ye what I have done to you? Ye call me Master and Lord: and ye say well; for so I am. If I then, your Lord and Master, have washed your feet; ye also ought to wash one another's feet. For I have given you an example, that ye should do as I have done to you. Verily, verily, I say unto you, The servant is not greater than his lord; neither he that is sent greater than he that sent him. If ye know these things, happy are ye if ye do them."

Now Jesus' teaching here is plain. Jesus was the Master and Lord of His disciples. He was their supreme Lord. Yet He took upon Himself the lowliest of menial duties — a task assigned to the lowest of slaves. And He did this because of the fact that He was teaching them that as their Lord, He had to become their Servant. His Lordship could only be exercised properly by becoming the lowliest of their slaves. And He did this when He suffered and died on the cross for them to take away their sins and secure for them washing by His blood.

But He laid down a fundamental principle of lordship here when He added: "Ye also ought to wash one another's feet. For I have given you an example, that ye should do as I have done to you." The point is that the disciples had to learn that to occupy a position of authority was *not* to occupy a position superior to others. The truth is the very opposite. To occupy such a position was to be a slave of those over whom they were placed. Then and only then would they properly fulfill their role in a position of authority. So it is always in the church. Officebearers are the servants and slaves of those over whom Christ places them. This is, from this viewpoint, an inferior position. If this were understood properly, perhaps there would not be all this silly propaganda for equal rights for women in the church.

So, Timothy, we come to the end of the argument. From every point of view, Scripture forbids women to hold office in the church. May God keep us faithful to His Word.

Fraternally in Christ,
H. Hanko

She Girdeth Her Loins with Strength

The Ways of Her House

A Virtuous Woman

Can a Woman Forget Her Sucking Child?

When Thou Sittest in Thine House

Abraham Kuyper

She Girdeth Her Loins with Strength

Back in the beginning of this century, Dr. Abraham Kuyper wrote a series of meditations on home life. These were subsequently published in book form, although in Dutch. In 1929 this book was translated into the English by Dr. John Hendrik DeVries and published by Wm. B. Eerdmans Publishing Co. under the title *When Thou Sittest in Thine House.* The book is long out of print, but it contains much pertinent material in it which is of value today to godly mothers. Several chapters from this book are reprinted here, all of them dealing with the work of a mother in the home.

She Girdeth Her Loins with Strength
Management of the Household

No, there is not alone *sickness* or *health*. There is still a *third* something. Something, that lies in between "health" and "sickness," and that sometimes already at an early age, follows us after as decline of strength; *weakness*.

"Nerves" it is called with one, "poverty of blood" with a second, with a third "exhaustion." But, by whatever it is caused, or to whatever cause it is attributed, the result is one. There lacks strength where strength ought to be. And the anxious feeling of not *being able* where one wants to do, comes back every morning, and to the exhausted man or woman continues as a plague until evening.

Especially woman, and not least married woman, *suffers* under this plague.

She became mother. What in Genesis 3 God laid upon Eve, that she should bring forth with sorrow, is also fulfilled in her. Thereby her constitution not overstrong already, suffered the more. And now the activities of life became too much for her. It went more and more above her strength. And while she tried to row against the stream, she became more and more worn out, till at length the weary head became so heavy, and the arm she would stretch out, fell almost helpless in her lap.

And though in this measure it is, thank God, the case with but a few, it is an almost *universal* phenomenon, that our housewives and housemothers, who are at the head of a somewhat busy household, frequently have no more strength of head and limbs for their difficult task of life, and that they themselves first, but also the family, and especially the children, suffer under this.

This distressing condition is even frequently aggravated by the fact that her daughters also lack freshness of vigor. So that, instead of supporting their weak mother, they themselves rather lean upon her.

And when the sons of the house also look pale, and need tonics, and instead of giving the impression of healthful virile strength, already at an early age begin to show shadows alongside of the unevennesses of the face; and also the man of the house complains; and as a climax of trial the very servants almost make you say, that as regards weakness of health they are part of the family, in the end it becomes too much for "mother," as on her rests the heaviest part of the burden of family cares, and many a housewife is at length carried out to the grave, because her busy household, in addition to her weak constitution, it is not too hard to say, had literally killed her.

* * * * * * *

To the danger that threatens the housewife from this side, the Proverb-poet also had an open eye, and therefore of the virtuous housewife he writes, that: "She girdeth her loins with strength, and strengtheneth her arms" (31, 17).

Just what the Psalmist sang of Jehovah; sang of the Lord of hosts, when he jubilated, that our God had clothed Himself with majesty and strength, and presently focused it all in this one note of joy: *He hath girded Himself.*

And because the Lord Himself "girdeth His loins," therefore it is He also, Who is able to stand by His beloved in their weakness, even as, in the very words of Solomon, in Psalm 89, 21, it is said to David: "With whom my hand shall be established; *mine arm also shall strengthen him."*

To gird the loins, is the perception, the feeling, the sensation of increase of strength, till you say to yourself: *Now I am able again.* And *to strengthen the arms* is to bring this restored strength into the arms, not now to be idle but to apply this regained strength after the Lord's ordinance.

This virtuous housewife girds the loins, not merely when with advancing years she becomes conscious of failing strength, but while as the picture of health she still directs the affairs of her household.

Of course this is figurative speech, and has nothing to do with putting on of a corset to feel oneself more firmly attired.

This girding is not done with a girdle which externally is fastened around the waist, but with a girdle of *will-power* and *self-control* and *prudent exertion,* which is woven in the inner chambers of the heart upon one's knees before God.

An imagery, which tells you, that this woman did not let herself will-lessly drift with the stream, did not let go of herself and did not succumb under her task, but consciously controlled the task, took hold of herself, exerted herself, and regulated the expenditure of her strength. Also that she took care in time, that when the lamp had burned many hours, fresh oil kept the flame burning, before it would die out.

* * * * * * *

Not *complain* and *sigh,* but *pray* and *give thanks,* and with courage in the eye face the life of each new day, is the precious effect upon the busy housemother of *quiet trustful faith.*

For faith is to live, not from what one sees before one's eyes, but from what one does *not see.* Hence after the rule, that not the *body* the soul, but the *soul* must govern the body, and that in cautious wisdom of the *understanding* and in steel-strength *of will* the weak woman has been equipped of God with two mighty weapons, wherewith to do battle against weakness.

Reports of healings by prayer are abroad again, especially in America. And the fact can not be denied, that by spiritual operations of faith, among Protestants as well as among Roman Catholics, remember Lourdes, healings have taken place, that make you think of miracles.

And yet these healings are nothing but the effect of will-power inspired by faith, concentrated upon one single point, which will-power, with higher strength, reacts against the appearance, that over against the body the soul stands impotent.

With cases of weakness one generally summons a physician, and who would despise the blessing of medicine. But it is a subversion of the Divinely appointed order, when the soul in you imagines that it stands impotent over against the body.

By all sorts of sins, also by unbelief, to a dreadful degree you can weaken your body and especially your nerves. But also by faith and an holier sense you can to so uncommon a degree strengthen this same body and these same nerves.

This is *girding your loins with strength.*

And the young married woman, who begins this early; who, with the increase of her family, uninterruptedly goes on with this, and never for a moment allows her family to run away with her, but calm and "strong in prayer" prepares herself for her task, will obtain the glorious experience, that in the midst of the distractions of a busy family-life godliness has a blessing also for her physical powers.

She who has neglected this and for years has brought her will into bondage to her nerves, and thus in old age reaps the bitter fruit of this, is of course not able to restore this wasted power by a single act of will.

But even then, it still holds true, that girding the loins with strength, by serious, prayerful exertion of faith, is the only means, to come away from under it. Even in such almost hopeless conditions, faith *never* refuses its strength-restoring operation.

* * * * * * *

Does this mean to say, that now the weak housemother may withdraw herself in the mystery, and neglect the outward means of support?

Of course not, for then it were purely the operation of the feeling and no healthy working faith.

No, faith knows *how* to apply means.

It knows that God Himself has not merely fore-ordained salvation for His elect, but at the same time and in that same counsel has ordered the *means of grace*, to bring about the salvation.

With mystery it must begin, but it must not stop therewith.

Faith fosters *wisdom*, which is something altogether different from school learning found in books.

You can so plan your household and so direct it, as to show lack of wisdom. But you can also do all this in such a way, that wisdom *shines out* from it.

There can be exhausting activity and confusion and disorder. But there can also be good rules, fixed procedure, steady direction and thereby beneficent order.

And in the measure in which this prevails in your household shall the use of your strength be either a wasting of the same, or a harnessing and effective application thereof.

* * * * * * *

Your strength is a gift of God, a *talent* entrusted to you.

This strength, this talent, must not remain what it is. It must be put to usury. Gains must be won by it. It must increase. And before God you must be able to say: "Three talents hast Thou give me, see Lord, three other talents have I gained therewith." And though as regards strength, you received but one talent yet this one talent must not be buried, but must be *doubled*.

But whether it is only just received, or whether it is already doubled by faithful discharge of duty, you must be sparing in the use of it.

It must not be *played with*. It must not be *wasted*. Self-control must direct all your doings.

There is division of time. There is division of the daily task. There is division of what you charge others to do. And not the woman who rushes along with things all day long and wears herself out, but the woman who, calmly seated in her armchair, plans the daily run of the household and tactfully directs its course, serves her God in her carefulness and radiates blessing in all her environment.

Even the matter of sleep, which increases strength, and regular meals, which feed the body, are to the believing woman parts of serious and regular performance of duty. She knows that the lamp, which receives no oil, gives out, and the hearth that is not continuously replenished. And therefore also sleep and feeding are no play with her, but a part of performance of duty and of obedience to her God.

To surrender a part of her housekeeping cares, that the whole slip not out of her hand, may at times be a demand of faith.

Nothing by way of material aid is to be despised, provided it renders her service, and she does not lean on it.

Upon God alone she must lean, and upon that *spiritual strength* of soul which God has granted her.

She alone who believes, not *sentimentally*, but *practically*, shall in this also be more than conqueror.

So in this struggle let the girdle of *faith* be the mystery of your strength.

The Ways of Her House
Care For the House

Of the good housewife the Proverb-poet writes, that she does not eat "the bread of idleness, for that she ever looketh well to the ways of her household" (31, 27).

There was a time, when especially in our large cities, some housemothers thought, that this looking to the ways of her house, referred to her care of the marble hall-ways, and when she knew, that the spotless flooring glistened with whiteness, as she had overseen the work of her maid, the reading of Proverbs 31, 27 gave her quiet self-satisfaction at the thought: "Such a woman who looks to the ways of her house, I am too."

This took place, even very frequently, in days of petrified piety, when many a housewife became very angry at seeing the least bit of dirt on the polished floor, but had no concern about the *baptized* maidservant, who had to clean it.

They were evil days, when the marginal readings of our Bible ceased to be read, and the beautiful interpretation of our fathers was forgotten: "The ways of the house here means, the whole course of *the household life,* so that the housewife keeps oversight over her *children,* over her *servants,* over the work that each has to do, and looks well to the *furniture,* and also to the *means* which her husband allows her."

This explanation was beautiful and rich, and at the same time made it plain, why there is added to it: *"and the bread of idleness she does not eat."*

This the woman does who prides herself on the spotlessness of her floors, and for the rest lets her household affairs go as they will.

But this doeth not the woman, who literally is busy from early morn till late at night, looking after all the interests of life in her house, to watch over and to direct them, and knows the ways of that life to its minutest particulars.

* * * * * * *

A pious and scholarly expositor added to this: "A good housewife does not remain seated in her chair, as though from the domestic throne to give out orders and instructions, but with her own eye she looks to the ways of her house, i.e., she has her hand in everything, and rules her house not as an officer by orders, but much more as becomes a careful mother, in person."

This does not mean, of course, that she gives *no* rule and *no* definite instruction. For where these are wanting, life loses its course. There things go haphazardly and slipshod, and domestic life makes no progress. You see this plainly in those neglected households, where one always drudges and is never done, and where endless confusion rather makes the impression as though one was ever on the *move*, instead of quietly *dwelling* in one's house.

Both are necessary. There must be fixed order in the life of the house. And that order must continue because the housewife continually has her eye upon it and is with it. Only then can you say: "*She looks to the ways* of her house."

And when you apply this to everything the marginal reading sums up, and to the order in which this is summed up, you need not fear, that such a woman will eat the bread of *laziness*. Rather the question rises, how this delicate woman stands it?

* * * * * * *

Consider, that the *order* in which the Annotator sums up her activities, is not: First the chambers, the furnitures, the money, and then the servants and the children. But reversely: first the children, then the servants, and only after that furnitures, money, and chambers.

The children come first. They are the live goods. The pledges entrusted to you of God, who have been baptized into His holy Name. And a housewife, who leaves her children to the care of a nurse, to a "bonne" or governess, that she herself might go out more freely, can take better care of her furniture, and more uninterruptedly keep at work on her embroidery, will bear her judgment of God, because she has neglected her duty as mother.

And though in the days when the marginal readings were put in the Bible, there was no social question as yet, even then in the estimation of our fathers the servants came *before* the furniture, chambers, and stairs.

Also servants are live goods, they are human beings, members of the church, baptized persons, and a housewife, who does not look to her servants, to care for them and to provide for their body *and soul*, shows that she does not understand what it means, that God has given her human beings in her service, that He has entrusted to her individuals that have a soul to lose.

Also what is added about "the means which her husband entrusts her with" is not considered by every housewife a matter of sufficient importance.

Also money is given of God. This also for His sake may not be carelessly handled. All money is *entrusted*, and therefore of *all* money we are accountable *to God*.

Two things only the Annotator forgot.

The housewife has also first to care for the *friends and guests of the house*.

Especially in the house with busy ways of life her task is thereby very comprehensive.

And in addition to this is the *husband*.

He too needs looking after. Not merely in clothing and food, but also in his way of life and formation of his character. And again, a housewife does not understand her calling, when she exerts no beneficial influence upon the formation and development of her husband's character.

* * * * * * *

Against this pious interpretation of the task of the housemother the spirit of our age meanwhile more and more opposes itself.

A woman who thus almost loses herself in the ways of her house, is scornfully looked down upon as a "house-sparrow." A woman should be vivacious, interesting, especially in social conversation. And, therefore, all this more ordinary life of the household, by way of a small barracks, must be finished by strict orders in the early morning-hour. For the rest it must be handed over to the servants, that the wife may have leisure to read, to play, or to go out, and to develop herself for a higher sphere of life.

According to God's Word the woman thereby *lowers* instead of raises herself.

Not as though the "house-dredge" is the Scriptural ideal. The sort of characterless women, who sink away in their household affairs and are nothing else than the copy of them, rather diametrically oppose the word of the Proverb-poet.

"To look well to the ways of her house" one must stand *above* it, occupy a higher viewpoint, and thus in spiritual contact live with that holier world, from which direction must come down with respect to the life of the household.

For a woman who fears God, the leading of the ways of her house is a matter of prayer.

For the "house-drudge" therefore we make no plea.

But when you ask what is of greater benefit to our people, and what advances the Kingdom of God more effectively, whether it is a woman's life that goes up in much reading, in much visiting, in much going out and for the rest in public "Christian activity"; or the life of a woman, that is bent upon being the warm and inspiring center of the domestic circle, upon devoting itself to bringing up the young and developing the older children, upon taking to heart the physical and spiritual well-being of the servants, and upon maintaining from house to house cordial friendly relationships between the families — who then hesitates to acknowledge, that the last by far the most interesting, creates the richest, the most noble womanly existence?

* * * * * * *

Undoubtedly life out of the house has certain conformableness to duty, but never otherwise than by receiving continually leading and direction from the center of the domestic life.

Everything out of the house that does not touch *your* heart, is abstract and barren. And according to God's ordinance your heart finds no other fireside, from which it can borrow its glow, than in the household thought-out of God, worked-out of God, created of God.

Where the household life is sound and healthy, you find people, old and young, who are healthy of heart.

And a people even as people never has more real strength, and as a nation can never take a higher standpoint, than when from the warm and inspiring home-life power and glow of enthusiasm stream out also in the veins of national life.

That so many serious-minded folk labor to stem this hand-over-hand increase of life out of the house in society, in coffee- or beer-house, is not because by itself there is evil in such a beer-house. But because by it the elasticity of the home-life suffers loss. And that loss affects injuriously the moral fiber of the rising generation.

As long as the household flourishes, everything is to be hoped.

Where the home-life begins to weaken, the worst is to be feared, not merely with respect to your national future, but even for your church-life.

And therefore there depends so much more than one can say upon the housewife.

According as *she* takes her duty seriously or lightly, she actually has in hand the welfare of the family-life, and through the family-life the future of the church and fatherland. And of this she will give account to God.

Account to God for herself, but account also for her daughters, how she has trained them, as women, for the task that awaits them in life and that mind and spirit she has developed in the female personnel of the house.

In those daughters of the family, provided the mother leads them aright, the good tradition of a former generation can be revived again, and so pass on upon those that come after, to the good of church and fatherland, to the benefit of all that are alive, and to the praise of the Name of our God.

But there can also be fostered in those daughters an *un*homelike, an *anti*-homelike spirit, which as an hereditary cancer enters into our families. And then it will be God, who will visit the sins of our duty-ignoring housewives by punishing them in the ways of their children.

A Virtuous Woman
The Housewife

Our translators do not speak in Proverbs 31, 10, of the "virtuous," but of the "real" housewife, and there is some difference here. In our times at least one thinks of a "virtuous" housewife as one who is reliable, good-natured, and home-loving; but he who speaks of a *real* housewife, means not merely an honest and good person, but one who is truly meritorious *as a housewife*.

And such was the meaning of the Proverb-poet.

In this beautiful song, in which Lemuel outlines the picture of the real housewife, almost no mention is made of the quiet virtues of this woman.

It says "that she feareth the Lord," but this, too, is not taken subjectively, but objectively. A woman who shows in her *housekeeping* that she does not pursue vanity, but feareth the Lord, she shall be *praised*.

For it says: "Favor is deceitful and beauty is vain, but a woman that feareth the Lord, she shall be praised."

There is even no appeal to verse 11: "The heart of her husband doth safely trust in her," as though this were said in praise of her marital faithfulness; for this word has nothing to do with it, and only means, that the head of the house is altogether confident, that his wife shall take good care of him. It states this literally and in so many words: "The heart of her husband doth safely trust in her, that he shall lack no good, i.e., not anything that he needs."

Overspiritual people will find this very prosaic; but such is Holy Scripture.

Does not Holy Scripture say of a minister or elder, that he who doth not know how to rule his own house, is worse than an infidel; which of course means to say that such an one injures the church of Christ more still than an infidel.

But actually the fundamental thought in both Old and New Testaments here too is one.

The *real* minister or elder must first rule his own house and then the house of God.

So the *real* housewife is evident first in this, and most in this, that she shows herself capable of taking good care of her house and of ruling it well.

* * * * * * *

The words themselves of the Proverb-poet indicate this.

That for which this genuine housewife is praised, consists of six things: first that she takes good care of her husband, second of her children, third of her maidservants, fourth of the poor, fifth of her goods, and sixth of her house.

She cares for *her husband*.

This stands at the head in verses 11 and 12 as her first marriage obligation: "The heart of her husband doth safely trust in her, so that he shall lack no good thing. She doeth him good and not evil all the days of her life."

Then she cares for *her children*.

Read it in verses 26 and 28: "She openeth her mouth with wisdom; and in her tongue is the law of kindness. Her children arise up, and call her blessed."

In the third place she cares for *her maidens*.

This you see in verse 15, where it reads, "She riseth also while it is yet night, and giveth meat to her household, and a portion to her maidens."

In the fourth place she cares for *the poor*.

"She stretches out her hand to the poor; yea, she stretches forth her hands to the needy" (v. 20).

This is her care for her *live* goods.

And this care for her live goods is so brilliantly crowned, that her husband and her children receive honor in the gate of the city; and that every one in the gates praises her by reason of the works of her hands.

* * * * * * *

But this does not satisfy her.

The largest place in Proverbs 31 is devoted to her care of her *goods* and her *house*.

Especially for her goods.

In the house there must be provisions, there must be supplies, and abundance of all sorts of goods.

And this genuine housewife did not harbor the idea, that her husband must earn everything, and that she needs but live on his money; but she herself was diligent, she worked in the hours which she saved to prepare wares for sale, and these she did so well, that they fetched high prices, and thus brought in gains, even to the extent that she was able to lay by and buy herself a field.

She spins and embroiders and makes ornaments.

Read it in verses 13 and 14: "She seeketh wool, and flax, and worketh willingly with her hands; she is like the merchant's ships; she bringeth her food from afar."

After that again in verses 19 and 22: "She layeth her hand to the spindle, and her hands hold the distaff. She maketh herself coverings of tapestry; her clothing is silk and purple."

And these products of her hands she *sells*. See it in verses 17, 18, and 24: "She girdeth her loins with strength, and strengtheneth her arms. She perceiveth that her merchandise is good; her candle goeth not out by night. She maketh fine linen, and selleth it; and delivereth girdles unto the merchant."

And with that merchandise of what she herself spun and embroidered she is so prosperous, that she lays by a small fortune.

So says verse 16: "She considereth a field, and buyeth it; with the fruit of her hands she planteth a vineyard."

* * * * * * *

And what finally concerns her care in narrower sense for *house* and *household*, in this too she does excellent work.

She wastes no time in sleep, but works evenings longer than it is day, and in the morning she is the first out of bed.

As it tells in verse 18: "Her candle goeth not out by night"; and in verse 15: "She riseth also while it is yet night."

Neither does she leave the care of her house to her servants, but she herself giveth meat to her household. Read it in verse 15: "She giveth meat to her household, and a portion to her maidens."

She is most careful too as to her own personal appearance: "Her clothing is fine linen and purple. Strength and honor are her clothing," which means, that she wears articles of good quality, and knows how to do this with taste and good form.

She has an eye to the whole house, the halls, the garrets, and the cellars. She is always busy. "She looketh well to the ways of her household, and eateth not the bread of idleness."

Yea, to add this to it also, she cares not only for her goods and for her household, but also for the house itself.

As it says in verse 21: "She is not afraid of the snow for her household; for all her household is clothed with scarlet," something that is to be understood of Eastern houses like this, that when there was no paper yet, the walls were hung with tapestries; and this was done with double thicknesses in winter, that the indoors might be the warmer.

All this the Proverb-poet adds together as marks of an housewife that feareth the Lord, and who for the sake of the fear of the Lord responds to her high calling as mistress of the house.

* * * * * * *

Lemuel does not draw this picture of a woman of the middle class or of a woman of the lower ranks of society, but of a woman of years in the high walks of life. For it says that *King* Lemuel thus drew the image of a woman for his son.

This was not yet the Christian woman, but a Jewish woman, who lived in the fear of the Lord.

And he who in the days of the Reformation takes the Christian woman at her best, knows in how serious and substantial a way the real housewife acquitted herself of her task as wife to her husband, as mother to her children, and as mistress of the house to her servants.

So was, and sometimes still is, the real housewife, to whom God grants, according to verse 25: *"to rejoice in time to come."*

That not every woman can be like this, is granted.

Not every woman has this physical strength and welfare at her command. Not every woman is endowed with such strength of mind, wisdom of insight, and admirable power of will.

And He who knows the talents of every one, here too shall pass a righteous judgment.

It must also be granted, that with present-day factories and stores, a woman is now no more able by her spindle and embroideries to lay by competencies.

With the change of times this too is altered.

But when the genuine housewife in old times so cared for her husband, children, and servants, and then had time left by spinning and embroidering to earn enough money to buy fields, how much greater should be the care for husband, children, servants, and houses now, when the "real housewife" is under no more necessity to embroider for trade, and is able to give all her time to her household!

You realize, that the task and calling of caring for the interests of the home is so much the more urgent.

And in these days so many fall short in this, who, alas, thereby stand behind even this Jewish housewife.

And when by reason of this the reading of Proverbs 31 sends the blush to the cheeks of many of our women, is there then no cause for laying hold of oneself in the fear of the Lord, and of doing what it says in verse 17: "She girdeth her loins with strength, and strengtheneth her arms"?

Can a Woman Forget Her Sucking Child?
The Mother

With a beauty that never pales, the prince of poets celebrated in song the tie, that binds the mother to her child, which she bore in sorrow, fed with milk at her breast, and had carried for so long under her heart, as that which "unites *the blood.*"

The estimate was correct. The love of mother for the child she bore does not spring from a tendency of soul, but from the blood, and therefore love in wedlock stands higher, because, "stronger is the tie of the couple, that, hand in hand, joined not to separate," for they love each other from inclination.

You need but to compare the world of our human life with the world of animals, to see at once the truth of this antithesis.

If the love of mother for her child were indeed the outflow of an higher inclination of soul and of self-denial, you would have to find this beautiful trait among people, but not among animals.

Yet the *opposite* is the case.

You find this love of her who was permitted to give life for what came to life frequently more strong with animals than with human beings.

Birds and domestic animals vie with one another to make exhibition of this, and already in early youth we read all sorts of interesting stories of little animal mothers, that sacrificed themselves for their young.

Yea, more still, even Holy Scripture has so high an estimate of this animal love, that in terms of it our Savior expresses His own love for His people, as when He compares this His love with that of a mother-hen, that covers her chickens with her wings, while on the other hand in Isaiah 49, 15, our God assumes at least the possibility of the human mother, that can forget her sucking child.

For it reads: "Can a woman forget her sucking child, that she would not have compassion on the son of her womb?" And then there follows: "Yea, they may forget, yet I will not forget thee."

Somber prophecy of what did happen, when it came to the

destruction of Jerusalem. For then, according to the dreadful historic narrative, in the insanity of hunger, mothers in Jerusalem killed their own sucklings, to feed themselves with their flesh.

* * * * * * *

Would you therefore count mother love for her child a small matter, and as something of minor importance?

You know that in more than one land, such as in France, and elsewhere, especially among upper classes, this love is ever more lightly counted. She who became mother soon abandons her child to the care of nurse and wet-nurse, and with many a mother all the concern with such a young child consists in this, that mornings and evenings she makes a short call at the nursery, or at times receives the beautifully dressed infant and makes a show of it in her luxurious drawing-room.

Even this some mothers deem too much. In France already two or three months after the birth there are many who send the little one far from home with a nurse to the country, that nothing may interfere with their pursuit of pleasure and enjoyment.

So in Paris, little mothers among animals do not act, but so frequently do they who become mothers among women.

Yea, there are those who purposely allow the milk in their breast that God gave them for their child, to dry up and disappear.

Thus in every sense there is reason, not to under-value the love of mother for her child, but rather to hold it high among us, lest with us also the practice gains foothold, which elsewhere is established to the shame of the name of mankind.

* * * * * * *

For the love of mother for her child is very like the love of an animal for her young, but it is also different.

With an animal love operates *exclusively* by instinct, is nothing but an impulse of nature, and shows itself therefore always in the same form and in the same way.

But so it is not with human mothers.

With our mothers this love for the child is a mixed phenomenon. It certainly springs from the blood. For no small part is instinct also common to her. But yet with the mother it is bound and subjected to the control of her moral life.

Not the animal, but she, can abandon her child to others or neglect it. And also, not the animal, but she, can carry that love up higher, ennoble and sanctify it.

Here applies therefore the gift of distinction.

As regards the love of such a mother for her child, you have to distinguish between two component parts, on one side what God instilled into her mother-nature, and on the other side what she did with this.

For what is instilled in her by God, the honor is not hers, but His. This is the nature of all mothers, and common to all including domestic animals and birds.

By itself there is nothing noble in this, bears no moral character, and is absolutely no evidence of self-denial.

A young woman, who thus far lived exclusively for herself and vanity, and now having become mother, at once forgets her vanity, is interested in and by her child, and for months together nurses her child, lives for her child, plays with the child and enjoys herself, may thereby become accustomed to self-denial and weaned from vanity; but by all this strong mother-love she offers no proof yet in the least of moral devotion.

What she does, the mother-hen in her way does too.

In this therefore God is great, not she, and He alone is glorified, who increated this beautiful trait in the mother as in the animal. A trait, which commonly is even more strongly evident among primitive peoples, than among civilized nations, in the country more mightily than in our refined cities.

* * * * * * *

But what the animal lacks, the human mother possesses, namely: by reason of her moral nature, she can either direct this love and sanctify it, or go contrary to it and sin it away.

The latter she can do in either one of two ways: She can silence the voice of nature and commit her child to the care of nurse or governess; or she can let her love for her child degenerate into infatuation for her child, misuse her child as a doll, and by her passionate attachment to the fruit of her womb already from the first beginning spoil her child.

It can also be otherwise, and God be praised, among those who confess the Lord it frequently is otherwise.

A mother can also elevate and ennoble, what in her nature is common with the animal. With moral insight and tact she can take this trait of nature as starting point, to love her child *in the faith*. For God's sake and from an inner sense of duty she can devote herself to her children. And putting aside all maternal vanity and passion, she can so direct and train her child already in those first beginnings of life, as bears evidence of the rule of higher aim.

Then the mother sees in her infant not merely the fruit of her womb, but far more a little creature which by His wondrous power has been called into being, and by Him, the Father of spirits, has wondrously been embroidered in her womb.

Then in that young infant she sees not merely a bundle of soft and tender flesh, but a little human being, in which hides *a soul;* perchance one of God's elect, and therefore loved of God as the apple of His eye.

Then there is prayer for that infant before she sees it with her eye. Already during her carriage she avoids everything that can be of injury to her child. She struggles through her birth-throes holding herself fast to the God of her life, that if possible, she might bring forth her little one. After the birth there is thanksgiving and making great God's glorious name. As soon as circumstances permit she seeks Baptism for her darling. The urge of her soul and the desire of her heart is, that her child may bear the seal of the Covenant. And she prays, not merely that God will spare her darling, but rather, that He may impart wisdom unto her, to show her child that real, that substantial, that glorious love, whereby from the very beginning she may convey not merely impressions, but *good* impressions to her little one.

And so real mother-love far excels the love of the mother-hen for her chickens.

There is indeed a common point of departure, but what the mother-hen lacks, the human mother shows that she possesses, even an higher, a nobler, a holier love, which what nature merely began, in and through grace makes perfect.

* * * * * * *

And when finally it is asked, whether in Christian circles this higher, this nobler, this sanctified love bears rule, then there is truly cause for thanksgiving, but no less for complaint, and the reason of this backwardness for no small part is found with the mother of years, who gives her daughters in marriage, without having prepared them sufficiently for their task of life to come.

This is mostly left to take care of itself. It is thought that after marriage with the child true mother-love will come of itself. Training, direction, warning is here at least thought superfluous.

And then this very thing avenges itself.

The young mother is then presently so altogether infatuated and charmed by her first mother-wealth, that she can think of nothing else, and almost will-less abandons herself to the impulse and passion of mother-love, and excludes from this her faith and her high calling.

This, too, will become different and better.

When presently Holy Baptism will resume its place of honor in our midst, from this holy Sacrament the spiritual call will go forth, which will impart to mother-love in our midst another, a higher, a holier character.

Not to say: "My child that I have borne," but the testimony: "A little creature of God, that I have received from Him, and that must be consecrated to Him," shall obtain the higher keynote.

And God, whose is the blessing of children, shall become great again in the mother-heart.

Phebe: An Example for the Christian Woman

Herman C. Hanko

In a sermon preached in Hope Protestant Reformed Church of Walker, Michigan, on Romans 16:1, Prof. Hanko examines carefully whether this passage supports the idea of deaconesses. In concluding that it does not, he nevertheless finds in it strong encouragement for women to occupy their proper and God-given place in the church and home.

Phebe: An Example for the Christian Woman

> *I commend unto you Phebe our sister, which is a servant of the church which is at Cenchrea; that ye receive her in the Lord, as becometh saints, and that ye assist her in whatsoever business she hath need of you; for she hath been a succourer of many, and of myself also.*
>
> Romans 16:1-2

> *Who can find a virtuous woman? for her price is far above rubies. The heart of her husband doth safely trust in her, so that he shall have no need of spoil. She will do him good and not evil all the days of her life. She seeketh wool, and flax, and worketh willingly with her hands. She is like the merchants' ships; she bringeth her food from afar. She riseth also while it is yet night, and giveth meat to her household, and a portion to her maidens. She considereth a field and buyeth it; with the fruit of her hands she planteth a vineyard. She girdeth her loins with strength, and strengtheneth her arms. She perceiveth that her merchandise is good; her candle goeth not out by night. She layeth her hands to the spindle, and her hands hold the distaff. She stretcheth out her hands to the needy. She is not afraid of the snow for her household; for all her household are clothed with scarlet. She maketh herself coverings of tapestry; her clothing is silk and purple. Her husband is known in the gates, when he sitteth among the elders of the land. She maketh fine linen, and selleth it; and delivereth girdles unto the merchant. Strength and honour are her clothing; and she shall rejoice in time to come. She openeth her mouth with wisdom; and in her tongue is the law of kindness. She looketh well to the ways of her household, and eateth not the bread of idleness. Her children arise up, and call her blessed; her husband also, and he praiseth her. Many daughters have done virtuously, but thou excellest them all. Favour is deceitful, and beauty is vain; but a woman that feareth the Lord, she shall be praised. Give her of the fruit of her hands; and let her own works praise her in the gates.*
>
> Proverbs 31:10-31

There are two reasons why I have decided to preach to you on this passage from the Word of God. The first reason is that this passage is quoted by those who support the idea of women serving in the office of deacon. They do this because the word "servant" which is used in verse 1 can also be translated accurately and properly by the word "deaconess," so that the text would read, "I commend unto you Phebe our sister, which is a deaconess of the church which is at Cenchrea." There is no question about it that that is indeed a proper translation as far as the word itself is concerned. The question which we must face is this: is that a proper translation in this particular passage, or are the translators of our King James Version right when they translate that word by "servant"?

The second reason why I call your attention to this passage of Scripture is that it gives to us by the example of Phebe instruction as to the proper place of women in the church. Phebe occupied an important place in the church at Cenchrea, and this is included by the Holy Spirit in the Scriptures for our instruction. We must receive this Word of God as such because there are those who would argue that the whole of Romans 16 is not really, in the strictest sense of the word, the Gospel to the church. They point to the fact that the whole of chapter 16 is composed of greetings which the apostle extends to various friends in the church of Rome, and that therefore it has no real value for the church of today. We must not take that position, of course. The question is, if that position is correct, why did the Holy Spirit then put it in the Bible? The Holy Spirit knows what the church today needs. So, we have in this entire chapter also part of the Word of Christ to the church; and we have that also in the example of Phebe. So, I call your attention to this passage under the theme: Phebe.

Who She Is

The Scriptures do not tell us very much about Phebe. In fact, these two verses of Romans 16 are the only two verses in the whole of the Scriptures which refer to her, and the information that the Scriptures give us in these two verses is rather meager.

Nevertheless, in the first place, she is said to be a member of the church at Cenchrea. That is rather interesting. If you will take out your Bible a moment and look in the back of your Bible at the map which gives the missionary journeys of the apostle Paul, you will find on the left-hand side of your map the peninsula of Greece. The peninsula of Greece was divided into two main sections. The northern part is called Macedonia, in which were found the cities of Thessalonica, Philippi, and Berea. The southern part of that peninsula is called Achaia or Greece, and you will notice that in that part of the peninsula is to be found the church of Corinth; and just a little ways to the south and east of Corinth is to be found the city of Cenchrea, where there was a church and where Phebe had her membership papers.

Now that church at Cenchrea was evidently established at the time when Paul, on his second missionary journey, made Corinth the center of his labors. That was usually the policy of the apostle in his missionary work: to establish a certain center of work and then to branch out from that center into all the surrounding area to preach the gospel. This is why, for example, we read in the Book of Acts that in the time in which Paul labored in the city of Ephesus the whole of Asia heard the gospel. Ephesus was the center. The same thing was true of Corinth. Corinth was the center of missionary labor and the whole of Achaia heard the gospel, and the fruit of that was that a church was not only established in Corinth but in Cenchrea also. We read, in fact, in Acts 18:18 that the apostle Paul, when he had finished his work in Corinth, and prior to his journey to Jerusalem, stopped in Cenchrea to fulfill a vow which he had made, and in fulfillment of that vow he shaved his head.

In the second place, Phebe was not only a member of the church at Cenchrea, but apparently a woman of considerable means. That is implied, at least, in the fact that Paul says of her that she was a succourer of many, and of myself also. It is also implied in the fact that although she was a member of the church at Cenchrea, she had journeyed to Rome on business, and the apostle instructs the saints in Rome to assist her in whatsoever business she hath need of you. It is because of that that, from almost the second century on, the church has said that this Epistle to the Romans was carried by Phebe to Rome from Corinth; and that is why you have here in the chapter this commendation of her. If you would look at the end of the Epistle to the Romans, you would find there at the end this note appended, "Written to the Romans from Corinthus and sent by Phebe, servant of the church at Cenchrea." So she evidently also carried this letter to the Romans which Paul had written.

In the third place, however, and more importantly, the apostle calls her in the text "our sister." Now that is a very common expression in the Scriptures, as you know. The people of God, in their relationships to each other, were often called brothers and sisters. We ought to say just a word about that because that not only is a very important truth, but it really undergirds the instruction of the Scriptures in these two verses. When the Scriptures speak of the people of God as brothers and sisters, then the figure of speech which is implied is that the church constitutes a family; and that indeed in our earthly families where there are parents and children you have a certain reflection of that spiritual relationship that prevails in the church of Jesus Christ. In that family God is the Father. He is the Father in the first place because of the work of adoption whereby He makes His elect people legally His sons and His daughters. God is the Father of that family, in the second place, because of God's work of regeneration, according to which He so works that His people are born again a second time and are born into the family of God. In that family Christ is the Elder Brother because He is the firstborn. He is the firstborn already in the counsel of God. In the womb of the counsel of God, as it were, Christ is born first, emerges first, to prepare the way for all His brothers and sisters to follow. As the firstborn, He is the heir, the heir of all His Father's possessions, just as the firstborn in the old dispensation received the double portion. As the firstborn, He is the Lord of His brothers. He rules over them just as in the old dispensation the firstborn who received the birthright had the lordship over his brothers. The result is that all God's people are brothers and sisters only because of the work of Christ which He performs; and in Christ all God's people belong to that one glorious family of God. They are, therefore, brothers and sisters in that one household of faith.

    Now the important part of this truth is that, from that point of view, the Scriptures teach that men and women in the church of Jesus Christ are equals. Just as brothers and sisters in one family, in relationship to their parents, stand on a plane of equality, so also do all the saints. Peter speaks of the fact that men and women are fellow heirs of the grace of life; and that very work of salvation puts men and women in the church in that spiritual relationship on a plane of total equality. Women, too, are believers. They, too, have the anointing of Christ. They, too, along with men, are prophets and priests and kings in the family of God.

    Does all that mean, however, that this text teaches that Phebe was a deaconess? That is the question. I say again that if it is proper to translate this text, "I commend unto you Phebe our sister which is a deaconess of the church which is at Cenchrea," then indeed we must have women as deaconesses in the church of Jesus Christ. But is that true?

I'd like to ask you to take out your Bibles because we are going to look at a few Scripture passages in this connection. I want to call your attention, in the first place, to the fact that it is rather striking that there are only two places in the whole of the Bible where this word can properly be translated as deacon, apart now from the question of the translation of this text. The first such passage is in I Timothy 3:8-13 where the apostle in writing to Timothy lays down the qualifications for the office of deacon. That is one passage where the word must be translated "deacon." The only other passage is in Philippians 1:1 where the apostle sends his greetings to the church of Philippi and specifically mentions in that connection the bishops and deacons (bishops here referring to the elders) so that his greetings are sent especially to the officebearers in the church of Philippi. There are no other passages, apart from these two, where we know for sure that this word must be translated "deacon."

On the other hand, there are many, many passages in the New Testament Scriptures where this word cannot be translated deacon but must be translated simply by the word "servant." I want to have you look with me at two of them. The first is in John 12:26. These two are chosen almost at random, but if you look at John 12:26 you will find that the Lord says this: "If any man serve me, let him follow me, and where I am there shall also my servant be." Now that word "servant" is exactly the same word as is found in Romans 16:1, and it is perfectly obvious that you cannot possibly translate that word by deacon; it would not make sense. "And where I am there shall also my deacon be." So there the correct translation is "servant."

The second passage is Matthew 23:8-11. Jesus is once again talking here: "But be ye not called rabbi, for one is your master, even Christ, and all ye are brethren. And call no man your father upon the earth for one is your father which is in heaven, neither be ye called masters, for one is your master, even Christ. But he that is greatest among you shall be your servant." Now, once again, although the same word is used there which is used in Romans 16, the translation cannot possibly be "deacon"; it would not make sense. "But he that is greatest among you shall be your deacon" would be incorrect. Obviously the correct translation is "servant." So, the point is, and that is the point which needs to be stressed, that this word has a much broader meaning than simply referring to the special office of deacon in the church but can refer to anyone who serves others and is busily engaged in ministering to the needs of others.

That, however, it cannot refer to women is clear from I Corinthians 14. And I'd like to have you look up that passage too. Paul is talking in this chapter about good order and decency in the worship services and in the life of the church of Jesus Christ as she comes to institutional manifestation in the world. And in verse 34, this specific and concrete injunction is laid down concerning the life of the church, "Let your women keep silence in the churches, for it is not permitted unto them to speak, but they are commanded to be under obedience, as also saith the law." Now, that text is so clear and so conclusive that those who argue for women in the office of deacon simply write this off as referring to the church of Paul's day only, but as having no relevance any longer for the church of today. But I would like to call your attention to what the text itself says: this is not a matter of my personal judgment concerning how things ought to go in the church of Corinth, but this is a matter of the law. The law, the law which is normative, the law which is an expression of the will of God for all times, says, let your women keep silent in the churches.

Now, there are two points that we should notice about this, and the first point is this. The office of deacon as Christ has instituted it in the church is also an office that has only one calling, the calling to bring the Word of God. That is why the text in Corinthians covers the office of deacon, too. We must not say that the office of the minister of the Word is to bring the Word of God, but the offices of elder and deacon are not to bring the Word of God, as if they have another kind of work to do. We must not say that. That is not true. It is true that each one functioning in the office must bring the Word of God according to the unique character of his own office, whether that be the office of ministry, the office of government in the church, or the office of dispensing the mercies of Christ. But, nevertheless, each officebearer has authority only because he comes with the Word of God. That is why our Form for the Ordination of Elders and Deacons says that the work of the deacons is also to bring to the poor the comforting words of the Scriptures. All three offices share that in common, that they come with the Word of God to God's people. They do not have any authority at all apart from that Word. The very authority of their office rests in the authority of the Word! They have authority only because when they come with the Word they say to God's people, "Thus saith the Lord." Otherwise their office means nothing at all. And it is because of that that the Scriptures say, women must keep silent in the church. They must not speak the Word.

The second remark is this. I cannot for the life of me understand why women are so eager to get into office in the church. The argument is, of course, that those who occupy an office in the church occupy a superior position and that everybody else who does not hold that office is in a certain inferior position; and when, therefore, women are forbidden the office, they are consigned to a certain inferior position in the church. That is not true. We must not look at the offices that way. We have to remember that, according to the words of Jesus, it is just the other way around. When Jesus, in the upper room with His disciples just before He was crucified, celebrated the last supper with them, we read that Jesus washed His disciples' feet. And after Jesus had explained to Peter just what this was all about and had overcome Peter's silly objection because Peter had a wrong notion about this, then Jesus said to His disciples, "Do you understand what I have done for you? You call me Master and Lord, and ye do well, for so I am. And if I as your master and Lord wash your feet, so ought ye to wash one another's feet." And the whole idea is that Jesus Christ is the Lord and Master of His church. But as Lord and Master He became the lowliest of servants for all His people. He worked as a slave. And He did that by suffering and dying on the cross for His people. He became their servant, their slave, their despised slave by suffering and dying on the cross. And now Jesus says, Let that be a lesson to you in what it means to occupy a place of authority in the church. To occupy a place of authority does not lift you up to some kind of pedestal where you are exalted over your fellow saints. Oh, no, it does not! But to occupy a place of authority means very, very simply that you be a slave to God's people, the lowliest of slaves to God's people. We ought to get that straight once, that whole idea about putting women in a position of inferiority. There is nothing to that. It arises out of a terrible misconception of the office, as if an officebearer is some kind of a supreme dictator in the church, who can from his high pedestal rule over God's people. Oh, no, it is not like that at all. If we have the correct idea of what the office is all about we would not have so much of a problem with this question either.

So, the correct translation here in Romans 16 is indeed that Phebe was a servant of the church at Cenchrea. How was she a servant? The apostle does not say very much about that in the text. He speaks of the fact emphatically that she was a servant of the church, and he defines that in this way in the latter part of verse 2: "That she hath been a succourer of many, and of myself also." There have been all kinds of speculation about that. Some commentators take the position that the church at Cenchrea met in her house, that she made her living quarters available for the church until they had a building of their own. Others say that, because Cenchrea was nearer to the coast than Corinth, Cenchrea was a city through which passed all kinds of people who were coming from Corinth and going to Corinth, and Phebe opened her house to the saints who were passing through the city on the way to the seaport, and that she made her house a kind of hotel in which she cared for the needs of God's people who were traveling. Others say that in addition to these things she probably lived in a certain relationship to the apostle Paul which was similar to the relationship in which certain godly women lived to Christ, that is, that she cared for the apostle's needs. She saw to it that he had food to eat, that his clothes were washed and mended, and that his material needs were provided for.

The Instruction of Her Example

The text does not tell us any of this. All of these things may be true, but the Holy Spirit has chosen to leave this all out of the text, and not to tell us specifically what kind of work Phebe did. And the reason why the Holy Spirit is quiet about this is that He wants us to understand that Phebe is an example to godly women in the church in every age, in the particular station and calling in life in which God has placed them. If you read the Scriptures, already in the Old Testament, and throughout the New, you cannot help but be impressed with the fact that the Scriptures give to women in the church a most exalted place. In fact, and I say this with some hesitation because I must leave the application to the Holy Spirit in your own heart, but the Scriptures leave us with the distinct impression that especially in times of spiritual crisis when there were few or no men who were spiritually-minded enough to care for the church, the responsibility for the welfare of the church fell upon women, and they more than men saw to it that the church continued. It may very well be that that is a commentary on our own times. I think, for example, of the days of the judges, when the only man available to fight the battles of Jehovah was Barak, who was afraid to fight unless Deborah went along. He did not have the courage; he did not have the faith. He did not have the complete trust in God that was necessary to fight against foreign invaders; and he flatly refused to go unless a woman went with him. I think of the example of Hannah who prayed so earnestly for a son, and who had a husband who was spiritually stupid, who seemed to lack the least bit of spirituality, who could not understand why Hannah wanted a son so badly, and who in his stupidity and lack of spirituality said to Hannah, "What's the matter with you, woman? Am I not better to you than a dozen sons?" As if Hannah's desire for a son meant that she did not love her husband! He could not understand that Hannah's desire for a son was her profound concern about the promise of God and about the coming of Christ. He had no feeling for that. I think of the days of wicked Athaliah, when she seized the throne, an imposter (from the house of Ahab) on the throne of David; she proceeded forthwith to kill all the seed royal. There was not a man to be found in the whole nation that had the courage to stand up against her. And there was not a man that had the courage even to prevent her from slaughtering the seed royal until a woman, Jehosheba, at the risk of her life, took one little baby of the seed royal, and fled with him and hid him until such a time as he could be crowned king.

How often Scripture seems to impress upon our mind that in times of spiritual decline and in times of apostasy, the welfare of the church seems to rest upon the shoulders of godly and pious women.

The point is that the church of Jesus Christ recognizes the fact that women have an important place in the church, and that indeed the life of the church, her very spiritual vitality and welfare is dependent upon the presence in the church of godly, God-fearing, virtuous women, without whom the church cannot exist. In the family of God they have such an important place that without it the family of God suffers.

It is that way. I cannot by any means give you an exhaustive list of what the Scriptures teach concerning this. I want to call your attention to a couple of elements anyway. In the first place, the Scriptures make it very clear that the place of women is primarily in the home. I am, frankly, terribly disturbed about the fact that so many of our mothers work. There seems, from the viewpoint of the Scriptures, no question about it that if this persists in our churches, our homes are going to be destroyed, and if our homes go, our churches and our schools will go too. The home is the foundation of the church and of the school. But it seems as if women want to work nowadays because of the fact that they are dissatisfied and discontented with their God-given place in the home, and that the home and the work of the home seem to them an intolerable bore. The Scriptures do not present it that way. The Scriptures speak rather of the fact that there are few, if any, callings in all of life that are more noble than the calling that Christian mothers have to be busy in their homes in the bringing forth and nurturing of children. There has got to be, beloved mothers — and I speak to you now from the depths of my heart — there has got to be a special place in heaven for godly and pious and virtuous mothers, who are content to take that place which God has given them in their homes, and are content to bring up their children in the hard day-to-day work of caring for the needs of the family. I cannot do that work. And that God has enabled women to do that is a miracle of no little importance. They have a noble calling from God which will be rewarded greatly when these humble mothers stand before the judgment seat of Jesus Christ. And the benefits of their work for the welfare of the church is beyond evaluation. We cannot begin to understand the tremendous benefits which the church and the schools receive because of the patient work of these God-fearing mothers.

In the second place, the Scriptures speak of the fact that there is in this family of God a whole area of Christian charity and benevolence which is beyond and at the same time the support of the work of the deacons. Not all Christian charity in the church of Christ is done by the deacons. It cannot possibly be. But the saints mutually — and we have evidences of that within our own congregation for which we ought everyday to be thankful — there is an area in the church of Jesus Christ where the saints together bear one another's burdens, care for one another's needs, help one another when some saints are in desperate trouble. And that work of charity which characterizes the church as a whole is the foundation, really, of the work of deacons. The foundation! The deacons could not do their work unless there was this broad Christian charity which the saints constantly showed to each other. And in that particular work God has given women an especially important place because they have from God natures which can do that kind of work much, much more readily than men. They have sympathy; they have understanding; they have a charitableness of spirit that men simply do not possess. And God has therefore given them that calling in the church, without which the church would not be nearly as strong or as spiritual as it is. Originally, you know, even our Ladies' Aid Society was organized with that specific purpose. That is why they were called Ladies' Aid Societies, because those societies help the poor.

In the third place, I am reminded of that passage in Titus, Titus 2, which speaks of the place especially which older women occupy in the church — that is, the women whose families now are grown up and whose children have left home and have established families of their own. Paul writes about them as follows: "The aged women likewise, that they be in behavior as becometh holiness, not false accusers, not given to much wine, teachers (mind you, teachers) of good things." And here is how they must teach: "that they may teach the young women to be sober, to love their husbands, to love their children, to be discreet, chaste, keepers at home, good, obedient to their husbands, that the Word of God be not blasphemed." Is that not beautiful? In other words, these older women who have had much experience in the difficult path of being a good wife and a godly mother are entrusted with the responsibility of helping the younger mothers in the difficulties of their calling. The younger mothers have all kinds of problems, you know, being good wives, helping their husbands, bringing forth children. And those problems they cannot talk about to the deacons. They cannot even talk about those problems often times to the minister or to the elders. They are much too personal, much too intimate, to discuss with just anybody. Paul says, and the Holy Spirit says, God has put women in the church to take care of the younger mothers. With their sympathetic and kindly nature, and with all their experience, they may teach the younger mothers what they have to know.

The Attitude of the Church Towards Her

And so, we could go on. The point is that God has given to women, to virtuous and godly women, a place of excellency, of honor in the church, so that the very welfare of the church of Christ is dependent upon these godly women. And it is that which is the reason for the injunction that the church receive these godly women in the Lord, as becometh saints. That, too, begins in the home. Husbands must honor their wives. How many of you husbands pray for your wives? How many of you do? I mean at the table, when your wife is there, and your children are there. Then you pray for your wife, and you bring her needs before the throne of grace so that she may know and the children may know that she is held in esteem and in honor in the home, and that the work that she has to do is such a difficult task that it requires the abundant grace of God for her to perform her calling. How many of you do that? You should. And you should, by all your conduct in the home, make it very clear to your wife and to your children that the place which the mother occupies is a place of esteem, a place of honor, a place of respect, because of the tremendous importance of the calling which the Lord has given to her.

And so the church must also receive these godly women, as Paul instructed the church in Rome to receive Phebe. Never let it be said of the church of Jesus Christ that they hold down women. Because if that is true, the church is unfaithful. In the family of God in which God has called us to live in this tight-knit relationship of the spiritual family where we are all one by the Spirit of our Elder Brother, Jesus Christ, women have their glorious and exalted place by God's appointment, fellow heirs with us of the grace of life. The very welfare of the church of Christ is dependent upon faithful, godly women. May we as a church receive them from God with thanksgiving and encourage them in their work and assure them of the blessing of God which will rest upon their faithful labors. May God give us that grace that our congregation here may prosper.

Women in Church Office

Robert D. Decker

The question of the right of women to hold ecclesiastical office is dividing Reformed and Presbyterian churches throughout the world. In this lecture, delivered in the Protestant Reformed Church of South Holland, Illinois, Prof. Robert Decker shows that the question is basically a hermeneutical issue; i.e., what does one believe concerning Scripture's inspiration and authority? Believing that the Bible is the infallibly inspired Word of God, Prof. Decker clearly demonstrates that Scripture is specifically opposed to women in church office. Prof. Decker is professor of practical theology in the Seminary of the Protestant Reformed Churches.

Women In Church Office

What do you believe about this Bible? Do you believe that the Bible is the inspired Word of God and is therefore infallible? Do you believe that it contains no errors and no contradictions? Do you accept the Bible as the full and complete revelation of God in Jesus Christ, and thus as the only rule for your faith and practice? Do you believe that the Bible's teaching applies with equal force in every age and culture? Or do you believe that the Bible contains both God's Word and man's word — some of each? Do you believe that the Bible must be subjected to the same rules of interpretation as any other piece of human writing? Do you believe, therefore, that what the Bible says is bound by its time and its culture, and that this in turn means that what the Bible says does not always apply?

But, you say, what has this to do with the subject of tonight's lecture? I thought you were going to speak on the place of women in God's church; and here you are, asking all kinds of questions about the Bible. That is correct. That is my subject, and I intend to speak on it. But there is a very important connection here between what one believes concerning the Bible itself and what he believes concerning the place of women within God's church.

Let me explain by asking still another question. From where has the problem of the place of women in the church arisen? That this is a problem no one will deny. The general assemblies and synods of the churches were very busy with this question, and from the looks of things they will be so for some time to come. The theological journals and church magazines carry many articles both pro and con, though I think mostly pro. And several books are appearing on the subject. Women are enrolling in increasing numbers in the seminaries and some churches are ordaining them into office — the office of pastor, of elder, and of deacon. But the question persists, why? Why all the controversy?

For long centuries this was never a question in the mind of the church. The church simply assumed that the office was limited to men.

Why is there a problem with this now? I submit to you, Reformed Christians, that the answer is this: compromise. That is why. The church once more has accommodated itself to the world. We live in the day of women's liberation. Women's rights and the feminist movement are very much in the news. Women are clamoring for equality and seeking fulfillment, not in the home, not in rearing a family, but in the professions and jobs of the work-a-day world. The world says that wives are not subject to their own husbands and need not obey them. The world says marriage is a fifty-fifty proposition. The world says women may rule over men. And many of the churches have caved in to the pressure of the world and have compromised. And now, all of a sudden, we need women office bearers, women ministers and elders and deacons.

But there is the problem. The Bible, in language so plain that even a child can understand, forbids women from serving as ministers or rulers in the church. I am going to show you that. Careful, believing exegesis of the Scriptures will yield no other conclusion. One simply cannot find support for women in office in the Scriptures.

What then do they do who advocate that women must serve in office? They deny that the Scriptures apply in our times and our culture. They say that the apostle Paul, when he wrote in I Timothy 2, "I suffer not a woman to teach nor to usurp authority over the man, but to be in subjection," was influenced by his rabbinical background and training. Or they say that this word applied in the early New Testament days and in that culture, but it does not apply in our times. Today we ought to have women as well as men in the offices of the church as well as men.

Hence, another, more serious, much more serious, concession is made, this time to the modern, liberal denial of the inspiration and infallibility of the Bible itself. That concession is couched in high-sounding theological jargon. We must understand, they say, that the Scriptures are time-bound, or they are culturally-conditioned. We must understand that they speak to their times; and it is our task today in the interpretation of the Scriptures to discover just how the Bible applies to our day and just how it does not. Or we must get at the basic meaning of the words themselves by following the methods and rules of the new hermeneutic.

But I submit to you that all of this, in spite of the terminology, is simply a denial of the most fundamental tenet of our faith, the faith rekindled at the Reformation — the inspiration and infallibility of the Scriptures. *Sola Scriptura.* With this higher-critical view of Holy Scripture one can make the Bible say anything and everything. He can make it support any heresy or deny any truth. And that is exactly what is happening in our day. One's view of Scripture has everything to do with our subject tonight. And let me be perfectly clear — I believe that the Bible is the inspired and therefore infallible Word of God. I believe that its truths apply in every age and culture. It is the complete revelation of God. It means what it says. It is the only rule for the church's faith and practice. Everything in the church must be done decently and in good order according to the teaching of the Scriptures. And because I believe this, I do not come to you tonight with enticing words of man's wisdom. I am simply going to expound the Word in demonstration of the power of the Spirit. These Scriptures clearly set forth the proper place and beautiful calling of women in God's church.

Scripture Assumes That Men Shall Occupy the Special Offices

This is obvious in the first place from the relationship of Jesus with several women. Jesus took time to minister to the needs of women. For example, He cast seven devils out of Mary Magdalene. He ministered the gospel to the Samaritan woman at Jacob's well. He raised the son of the widow of Nain. And He freed the daughter of the widow at Sidon from a devil. Several women were very close to Jesus and enjoyed a warm and personal friendship with the Savior and took delight in caring for Him. The most prominent were Mary and Martha, the sisters of Lazarus. Christ made His first resurrection appearance to a woman, Mary Magdalene. Certainly therefore Jesus had time for women. He took sympathetic interest in their needs. He revealed Himself as the Savior to them. The Savior never lorded it over them. He never regarded those women as inferior to or of less worth than men. And yet, strikingly enough, the Savior called none of these women to the office of apostle, evangelist, pastor, elder, or deacon in the New Testament church.

The same is true of women in the early church. There were several women among the 120 upon whom the Spirit was poured in the upper room at Pentecost. We read often of the women of the church in the Acts record. It happened more than once that Paul preached to women. Several women served both the apostles and the people of God. There was Dorcas, or Tabitha, who is remembered as much for her being raised from the dead by Peter as for her being full of good works and alms deeds. Paul remembered the unfeigned faith of Timothy which dwelt first in his grandmother, Lois, and in his mother, Eunice. At the knees of these saints Timothy first learned the Scriptures. Lydia was the first convert at Philippi. Priscilla was of great help to the apostle Paul in his work.

One certainly, therefore, cannot accuse the apostles of mistreating or ignoring the women Christians or of allowing them no place in the church. The apostles honored the women of God. They spoke favorably of them, just as Jesus had done. They valued their service highly and they commended and encouraged them. But the apostle Paul and the rest of them never ordained a woman as pastor, elder, or deacon in the church. Women assisted the apostles, helped the poor, kept their homes, and instructed their children in the fear of God; but they did not preach, they did not rule, and they did not serve in the office of deacon in God's church.

That Scripture assumes that men shall occupy the special offices is evident from those passages which speak of the qualifications for the special offices — I Timothy 3 and Titus 1, for example. These passages speak of men, not women, as elders and deacons in the church. Among the qualifications are these: they must be the husband of one wife, and they must know how to rule well their own houses before they can rule the church. Those passages expressly do not say the wife of one husband. And that is because there simply was no question in the minds of the apostles and in the early church as to the Lord's will that men should preach, rule, and minister the mercies of Jesus.

But perhaps you object. Perhaps you say, "Did not women occupy office in the Old Testament church — Deborah and Huldah, for example? And was not Phebe a deaconess according to Romans 16:1-2?" But notice: if Phebe was in the office of deacon, she was the only woman to occupy that office in the New Testament. That she actually held that office is very unlikely in the light of the rest of the biblical evidence. It is true that the word translated "servant" in Romans 16:1

in the King James Version can be properly translated "deaconess." It is also true that this word is used to refer to the office of deacon in the New Testament. But we must bear in mind that the same word occurs in a host of other connections in the Bible — servants, male or female, who wait on tables; servants of kings; servants who must be obedient to their masters; servants of God who occupy positions in government. One cannot, in other words, simply conclude, on the basis of the term alone, that Phebe was a deaconess in the church. In the light of the rest of the New Testament, she could not have been. Rather, she was a godly woman who served her fellow saints in the church, who was remembered by the apostles, but who was not an officebearer. In the Old Testament, yes, there were prophetesses like Huldah, and leaders of armies like Deborah. Two things, however, are worthy of note. First, this occurred only during very bad times in Israel, times of great apostasy, like that of the judges, or of the captivity of Judah. Much to the shame of the men of Israel who were not fit for office, God had to raise up women. And, secondly, these are very obviously not the general rule but the exception, and quite rare at that.

Scripture Teaches the Headship of the Man and the Subjection of the Woman

We find this in I Corinthians 11, especially verses 3-16. The subject of this passage is not, first of all, what some think it is. The apostle is not speaking about the propriety or the impropriety of women wearing or not wearing hats to church. That is not the idea. The main subject here is the great principle of the headship of the man over the woman in God's church. With respect to the woman, this means that she must be subject to her head, the man. And this subjection of the woman must be evident also in her appearance, especially in the public meetings of the church.

Now then, we must bear in mind that the apostle speaks here of matters which have to do with the public worship of the church. This is evident from the reference to praying and prophesying in verses 4 and 5. It is also plain from the rest of the chapter, which deals with the proper administration and observance of the sacrament of the Lord's Supper. Finally, the chapters which follow, 12-14, deal with the subject of the worship of the church from the point of view of the gifts and offices of the Spirit of Jesus Christ. Specifically, therefore, the subject has to do with the place and proper appearance of women in the church. Thus, in verse 3, the apostle lays down the principle — the principle, mind you, which is determinative of the practice which the rest of the passage enjoins. That principle is stated in the form of three assertions. Notice: the head of every man is Christ; the head of the woman is the man; the head of Christ is God.

The figure of the head is used extensively in the New Testament. The head is that upon which the body is dependent and to which it is subordinate. In this sense Christ is said to be the Head of the body which is His church.

That is true from two points of view. In the first place, organically Christ is the Head of the church as the life of the church. Through faith the church lives out of Jesus Christ and receives all her life and being out of her Head, Christ. And, in the second place, in the judicial or legal sense Christ is the Head of the church as its Lord. Christ is the authority of the church, and the church is subject to the rule of Jesus Christ.

This latter, the legal or judicial sense, is the meaning here. That Christ is the Head of every man means that He is the supreme Ruler, the absolute Ruler, of every man. And every man must therefore be in subjection to Christ. Man must not stand above Christ but be in obedience to Him.

But the head of the woman, the apostle immediately adds, is the man. The meaning is plain enough, is it not? If Christ be the Head, that is, the Ruler of every man, and man must be therefore subject to Him, is it not perfectly plain that the headship of the man over the woman must mean that she must be subject to the man? The woman must not stand over the man. She always stands in subjection to the man. The man is the head of the woman, and not the other way around. Already the point is obvious. The woman rejects her God-given, proper place, as well as her calling, when she rules over the man in the church of Jesus Christ. The woman who becomes pastor, elder, or deacon assumes a responsibility and usurps an authority which simply does not belong to her according to the plain teaching of the Word of God. By so doing, a woman occupies a place God never intended for her. And, of necessity, she refuses to serve in the beautiful place which God *has* ordained for her.

That this is the meaning is evident from the last statement of verse 3: "The head of Christ is God." That simply means that Christ, not the second Person of the holy Trinity now, but Christ as the Mediator, is always subject to the will of His heavenly Father. His Word is: "I come to do thy will, O God." Thus, the principle taught in the passage is: the head of the woman is the man. The head of the man is Christ. And the head of Christ is God. The relationship is such that in being subject to the man, her head, the woman is subject to Christ, Who is subject to the Head of all, God Himself.

This relationship is further explained in verses 7-12. Verse 7 teaches that the man is the image and glory of God. But the woman is the glory of the man. Man as image bearer of God reflects something of God's glory and majesty as the head over all things in Jesus Christ. The man is the image and glory of God exactly as the head of the woman. And the woman, who was herself created in the image of God, reflects that image of God precisely in her place as the glory of the man.

There is nothing demeaning or disgraceful about this. No more than it is disgraceful for Christ to be subject to God, or for the man to be subject to Christ his Head, is it a shame or is it a disgrace for the woman to be subject to her head, the man, and in him and through him to Christ and in Christ to God. That does not mean that the woman is inferior or of less worth. That simply is the role, the place, which God has given her. To say that this is demeaning to her is to contradict the Scriptures, which everywhere honor the women of God's church in their God-given place. This position, that of being subject to her head, the man, is the lofty and beautiful place God has assigned to the woman, a necessary place for her. And notice this, here the woman functions as woman with her gifts and her talents from the Spirit of Christ, in the midst of the church, for the edification of her fellow saints and for the glory of God.

Shall we pretend, I ask you, to be wiser than God by forcing the woman into a place of authority over the man? The apostle states the ground in the next two verses. They read: "For the man is not of the woman but the woman of the man. Neither was the man created for the woman but the woman for the man." That is plain enough, is it not? The apostle appeals to creation itself. Adam was created first, and Adam was incomplete. He lacked something. He lacked a wife.

Genesis 2 teaches us that there was found no help meet for Adam. So, for Adam's sake, to fulfill his need and his lack, God made the woman as his complement. Literally, therefore, the woman is *out of the man*, from his rib. As Adam exclaimed, "Bone of my bones and flesh of my flesh, she shall be called woman, for she was taken out of man."

But let there be no misunderstanding of the implications of this relationship between the man and the woman. Verses 11 and 12 remind us: "Nevertheless, neither is the man without the woman, neither the woman without the man in the Lord." That is important, very important. "For as the woman is of the man, even so is the man also by the woman," the apostle writes. Note that the principle of the headship of the man nevertheless remains, for neither is the woman apart from the man, for the woman is out of the man. The woman must be subject to the man. The man is her head.

But, this headship of the man in no sense destroys the interdependence of the man and the woman in God's church. Why not? Nor is the man without the woman in the Lord. And the reason is that the man is through the woman. Every man after the first man Adam is born of a woman. Without the woman, therefore, there can be no man. He simply cannot exist. And all this is of God, for all things are of God, the apostle says. Let no man imagine that he can stand apart from the woman. It remains forever true: the woman was created out of the man, so she must be subject to her head the man. But it is equally true that the man is through the woman and cannot be the head of the woman and the image and glory of God except through the woman. Hence, in the Lord there is perfect unity of the woman and the man in the church. The woman needs the man, but the man also needs the woman. Neither stands independent of the other. In the Lord they are together, they are one, and they need each other.

Let no man think, therefore, that because he is the head of the woman, he may exercise harsh tyranny over her. Let him never think the woman has no meaningful place in the life of the church. Let him never, in sinful pride, regard the woman as inferior and of no worth in God's sight. The fact remains, neither the man nor the woman is without the other in the Lord. This therefore is the principle taught in this passage: the man is the head of the woman, the woman must be subject to the man, the man is appointed to rule as head. Thus, in their proper relationships together, they reflect the image and the glory of God.

This of necessity means that the woman may not rule over the man in the office in God's church. This principle never changes. You may say what you will, but this is what I Corinthians 11 teaches. It is the unalterable truth concerning the relationship between the man and the woman in God's church. It is not something conditioned by culture or bound by time. It simply cannot be that in the New Testament times the headship of the man applied, but in our day the man and the woman are equal. Nonsense! The woman is ever subject to her head, the man, in the church of Jesus Christ. She may never rule over him. She may not occupy, therefore, the office of minister or elder or deacon. You find the same principle, by the way, applied specifically to the marriage relationship in Ephesians 5.

Scripture Expressly Forbids Women to Occupy the Offices of Christ

There are two passages which teach this. The first is I Corinthians 14:34, 35 which reads: "Let your women keep silence in the churches, for it is not permitted unto them to speak, but they are commanded to be under obedience as also saith the law. And if they will learn anything, let them ask their husbands at home for it is a shame for women to speak in the church." This passage is so utterly simple that it hardly needs explanation. The woman must keep silence in the church. That means she is not allowed to speak. And that speaking must be taken in the sense of preaching and teaching the edifying Word in God's church, i.e., in the sense of the official ministry. This the woman is not allowed to do. It is not at all unlikely that among the abuses in the Corinthian church was this, that the women were being allowed to participate in the leading of the worship service. This is not permitted, says Paul, for the woman is commanded by God to be in subjection. Hence, let the women keep silence in the churches. Indeed, it is a shame for the women to speak in the churches. A shame, mind you!

The second passage is I Timothy 2:11, 12. "Let the woman learn in silence with all subjection. But I suffer not a woman to teach, nor to usurp authority over the man, but to be in silence." Again, let us keep in mind the subject here. The apostle is speaking of the official worship of the church of Jesus Christ. The church, its offices, its worship, the various qualifications for office, the duties of ministers, elders, and deacons — all these are the subject of the first letter to Timothy. Hence, the apostle is not speaking of the woman's place in the home or in society but of her calling in the church of Christ. She must, for example, teach her children at home, to be sure, and she must rule them too. "Therefore, I suffer not a woman to teach" means in the church. A woman is forbidden to occupy the pulpit of the sanctuary. A woman may not be ordained to the office of the ministry of the Word.

And secondly, nor may the woman usurp authority over the man. Notice, this term literally means "to act on one's own authority, to be autocratic." And again, Scripture means in the church. The woman may not occupy the ruling office of Christ in the church, that of elder. A woman who does so is a usurper. She acts, not on God's authority, but on her own authority. Rather must the woman learn in silence with all subjection. She must learn, learn the truth, and grow in the knowledge of God, by means of the preaching of the Word.

And she must learn in silence, literally in quietness. And that means a bit more than just not talking, though it is that too. But "in quietness" means that it is in "tending to her own affairs and in her own God-given place and beautiful task" that the woman must learn. She must not meddle into the affairs which God has assigned to the men of the church.

Still more, she must learn, the apostle writes, in silence with all subjection. Subjection, plainly, is obedience. And *all* subjection is *total* obedience. In this way she must learn in silence, in total obedience to the Word and will of God.

And the ground or reason is twofold. The apostle appeals to creation, first of all, just as in I Corinthians 11. Adam was first formed, and then Eve. The woman was made for the man and not the man for the woman. And, secondly, Adam was not deceived but the woman, being deceived, was found in transgression. Now that cannot be understood to mean that Adam did not fall. We know better, of course. Adam, however, was not deceived in the way that the woman was deceived. The woman was utterly and completely deceived, for she was the leader in the fall, the one who talked with the devil and the one who became the occasion for Adam to fall. She listened, she talked, and she gave to her husband. As a consequence, God said, already way back in Genesis 3:16: "Thy desire shall be to thy husband and he shall rule over thee."

Scripture Calls Women to Their Proper Place and Task — Child-bearing

I Timothy 2:15 says: "She shall be saved in childbearing." That is the unique, the beautiful, the glorious place that God has given women within His church. She shall be saved in child-bearing. That needs all of the emphasis we can give it, especially today. That includes the actual conception and giving of birth and the rearing of children.

God gives women all kinds of opportunities to teach and to rule their little ones in the fear of His name. And what a glorious task that is! What a beautiful place God has given to women! Unto this end God has blessed the woman with many gifts and virtues which fit her physically, emotionally, and in every other sense for her beautiful place — gifts God has given her which the man does not share. Think of it. In this way God's church is born into the world and gathered. In this way Christ came into the world. Born of a woman, the Bible says. God did not need and He did not want to use a man. Can there be anything more wonderful than to be used of God for the building of the church? What a heinous sin when women, and men with them, refuse that calling by means of birth control or by the cold-blooded murder of abortion. The judgment of God rests upon them. For with fists in the face of God, they refuse to occupy the place which God has given them — the beautiful and glorious place of bringing His church into the world.

Through child-bearing she shall be saved, mind you! Oh yes, by the blood of Jesus through faith in His name, to be sure, but in the way of child-bearing. Not in the way of teaching, not in the way of preaching, not in the way of ruling in God's church, but in the way of child-bearing.

What about women to whom God does not give this privilege of bearing children? Have they no place? Oh yes, they do. A wonderful place. Let them be known after the example of the women in Scripture for their being full of good works and alms deeds, as Dorcas of old. Let them visit the fatherless and the widows in their affliction. Let them assist the poor, and be involved in helping God's church. But let them not stand in the place of men. Let them labor with their God-given abilities for the cause of Jesus Christ. Let them stand in the place of the parent in the Christian school to give instruction to the children of God's covenant, but let them not be elders or ministers or deacons. That the Scriptures plainly do not allow.

Before I state the conclusion, we have to look at Galatians 3:28, because it is invariably cited as proof for having women in church office. The text reads: "There is neither Jew nor Greek, there is neither bond nor free, there is neither male nor female (that is the clause, of course), for ye are all one in Christ Jesus." Let it be understood that this text has absolutely nothing to do with the question before us tonight. The passage makes plain that there is only one seed of Abraham, those who are chosen in Christ and united to Him by faith both in the Old and the New Testament eras. No matter who they are, these are the seed of Abraham. There is only one promise. And that one promise is Christ. The law cannot disannul or make of no effect that promise because Christ has removed the curse of the law by becoming a curse for us. There is only one way of salvation, the way of faith in Jesus Christ. And if you are in Jesus Christ, the apostle says, it does not make any difference whether you are a Greek or a Jew, whether you are a slave or a free man, whether you are a male or a female. If you are in Christ by faith, you are an heir of the promise. That is all. It does not have anything to do with women serving in office.

Hence, the Scriptures are clear enough. The woman is not permitted to preach, rule, or minister the mercies of Christ in the offices in God's church. That is I Corinthians 11. It is I Timothy 2. It is I Corinthians 14 and all of Scripture. And, I submit to you, either you believe that and you walk according to that or you reject it — the plain teaching of the Word.

One thing is sure. One cannot argue on the basis of these passages that women are permitted to enter into the office of Jesus Christ in the church. The only position left then is the one which so many are taking. We must regard these passages as merely the words and opinions of the apostle Paul — time-bound, culturally-conditioned, and not in force in our time or in our culture. Paul was following rabbinical methods of expounding the Old Testament. Then you have to say, you see, that in the Bible you have both God's Word and man's word. But I submit to you that the moment you say "*both/and*" you will have only the "*and.*" You will have nothing left of the Word of God. And when you have lost God's Word, my friends, you have lost everything.

The fact remains that these passages do not allow women to serve in office. This has been the position of the church for many centuries. Now to say that women must serve in office in the church is to say that the church has been wrong for all these many centuries! And that, in my opinion, is stinking pride.

Let me ask you once more: What do you believe about this Bible? The apostle Paul in I Timothy 2 says: "I speak the truth in Christ, I lie not." What do you say? Are you going to say that the apostle Paul spoke the lie when a few verses later he says: "I suffer not a woman to teach nor to usurp authority over the man"? I, for one, do not dare to say that. I believe this Word of God. Do you?

The Calling of Women in Church Office

Ronald Cammenga

Rev. Ronald Cammenga, pastor of the Loveland Protestant Reformed Church in Loveland, Colorado, examines carefully the biblical data on the place of women in the church. His analysis of the Scriptures leads one to the inescapable conclusion that the Scriptures, while forbidding women to hold ecclesiastical office, have an important place for women in the church.

The Calling of Women in Church Office

To say that this subject is a live issue in the church world of our day is to state the obvious. Certainly the role of the woman is a much discussed issue in the world at large, and especially in modern American society. We live in the day of women's liberation, women's rights, and the feminist movement. Women are clamoring for equality with men and are seeking fulfillment, not in the home and not in raising a family, but in the professions and careers traditionally occupied by men. The women's movement has become highly organized, a political force to be reckoned with. An organization like NOW (National Organization for Women) is devoted to political action and the spreading of propaganda on behalf of the women's rights movement. All across our country organizations traditionally open only to men, from high school soccer teams to the Jaycees, are being pressured to admit women.

It is not surprising, therefore, that there is also a parallel movement in the churches pushing for the admittance of women into the special offices, the offices of minister, elder, and deacon. The general assemblies and synods of the churches have been very busy with this question in the last few years, and from the looks of things will continue to be occupied with the issue for some time to come. The theological journals and church magazines carry many articles, both pro and con, on the question. Several books have been written on the subject. Women are enrolling in increasing numbers in the seminaries. And many churches, some with and some without the approval of the broader assemblies, are actively ordaining women into the offices.

We want to consider here this question of women in church office. At the outset, we want to clear up a common misconception and misrepresentation. Often the two sides on this issue are divided into those who are "for" women and those who are "against" women. The position "for" women means that women can do anything men can do, may hold any office that men may hold. All possible distinctions are to be erased. The position "against" women means that women are not allowed to do all that men do, are not allowed to hold every office that men hold, and are called to be in submission to the man in the home and in the church.

At best this is a serious misconception: at worst it is a deliberate and malicious misrepresentation. It is our conviction that the Bible does not allow the woman to hold every office that the man holds, and that the woman is called to be in submission to the man in the home and in the church. But this is not a position "against" women, but a position "for" women, really the only position "for" the women. The Bible is "for" women, that is, the Bible has the woman's own best interests in view and prescribes what is best for the woman herself. Exactly because the church is motivated by the good of the women themselves, the church must be committed to adhere to the Bible's teaching on the question of women in office.

The Biblical Position on This Question

The Bible prescribes a large and important place for women in God's church.

This is plain, first of all, from Jesus' relationship with several women. Jesus was interested in and took the time to minister to the needs of women, and not once did Jesus treat women in a demeaning way or regard them as inferior. He cast seven devils out of Mary Magdalene. He preached the gospel to the Samaritan woman at Jacob's well. He defended and forgave the woman taken in adultery. He raised the son of the widow of Nain, and freed the daughter of the Syro-Phoenician woman from a devil. Several women were especially close to Jesus and enjoyed a warm, personal relationship with the Savior. The most prominent of these were Mary and Martha, the sisters of Lazarus, and Mary Magdalene. The women were, strikingly, the last to leave the scene of Jesus' crucifixion and were the first ones to whom the gospel of the resurrection was preached. The Savior, however, called none of these women to be one of His twelve disciples nor later sent any of them out as one of the apostles.

This same large place is accorded women in the early church. There were several women among the 120 disciples in the upper room when the Holy Spirit was poured out on the Day of Pentecost. We read often of the women of the church in the record of Acts. Several women served

The Calling of Women in Church Office

both the apostles and the people of God. There was Dorcas, or Tabitha, who was raised from the dead by Peter, concerning whom we read that she "was full of good works and almsdeeds" (Acts 9:36). The first convert of the apostle Paul at Philippi was Lydia, the seller of purple. Paul remembered the unfeigned faith of young Timothy, which dwelt first in his grandmother Lois and in his mother Eunice. From these godly women, Timothy had first learned the Scriptures, II Timothy 1:1-5. Priscilla, along with her husband Aquila, was of great help to the apostle Paul in his missionary labors.

One certainly cannot accuse the apostles of mistreating women, or of ignoring women, or of allowing women no place in the life of the church. They honored the women and spoke highly of them. They valued their services and encouraged and commended them highly. But the apostles did not ordain women into the offices of minister, elder, or deacon. These women assisted the apostles, cared for the poor, instructed the younger women, kept their homes, and reared their children in the fear of God, but they did not preach, they did not sit in the elders' bench, and they did not serve in the office of deacon.

This important and large place which the Scriptures give to women is in keeping with the Scripture's teaching on the equality of the woman with the man. The Scripture's teaching that the women is to be in submission to the man and that the woman is "the weaker vessel" does not take away from a certain equality of man and woman.

This indicates that the whole question of women in office is not a question of the woman's equality with man. Equality and difference of role are not mutually exclusive. In fact they are two aspects of Scripture's teaching on this issue.

There is a certain biblical equality of the woman with the man. The creation already brings this out: both man and woman are created in God's image, Genesis 1:27; and God's command to exercise dominion over the creation comes to both the man and the woman, according to Genesis 1:28. The fact is that in the very passages in the New Testament which teach the headship of the man over the woman there always appears a statement about their equality and mutual dependence. The Scriptures are very concerned to guard against the headship of the man being interpreted to justify a harsh, tyrannical, domineering rule of the man over the woman. So we read in I Corinthians 11:11, 12: "Nevertheless neither is the man without the woman, neither the woman without the man, in the Lord. For as the woman is of the man, even so is the man also by the woman; but all things of God." The man is out of the woman, depends upon the woman, is called to live all his life through the woman. In I Peter 3:7 the apostle exhorts, "Likewise, ye husbands, dwell with them according to knowledge, giving honor unto the wife, as unto the weaker vessel, and as being heirs together of the grace of life; that your prayers be not hindered." Men and women are "fellow heirs" of God's grace and of eternal life.

The Scriptures teach that men and women are equally involved in ruin. Men and women stand equally in need of salvation. Jesus Christ is the Savior alike of women and men. Men and women alike possess the Holy Spirit of Jesus Christ, and therefore equally share in the office of all-believer, the office of prophet, priest, and king. As Joel had prophesied, the Spirit was poured out not only upon Israel's sons, but also upon her daughters, Joel 2:28, 29.

The Biblical Prohibition of Women in Office

Although all of this is true, the Bible forbids women to occupy the special offices in the church. Any fair and honest treatment of the biblical material will yield no other conclusion, as the church up until recent times has maintained. What is that biblical material?

First of all, the history of the Old Testament reveals very clearly already God's will that the leadership and offices in His church be entrusted to men. The leadership roles in the Old Testament were consistently assigned by God to men. Noah was called by God to build the ark and lead the church out of the old world and into the new world after the Flood. It was the patriarchs, Abraham, Isaac, Jacob, and Jacob's twelve sons who led the church in the period after the Flood. It was the man Moses who was called by God to deliver Israel out of Egypt and lead them to the Promised Land. And it was Joshua who was appointed by God actually to bring the children of Israel into the land of Canaan.

In the Old Testament God assigned the office of the priesthood to Aaron and to the male members of his family, and not one woman was ever called to the priesthood. There were also elders throughout the Old Testament and right into the New Testament, but there is no mention ever made of a woman's being among the elders of any city in Old Testament Israel. Neither did a woman ever occupy the throne in Israel, except the godless usurper Athaliah, who was eventually killed by order of the God-fearing priest Jehoiada.

This male leadership of the church continued into the early New Testament. The Lord Jesus called twelve men, not six men and six women, to be His disciples. Peter, led by the Spirit, called the 120 believers in Acts 1:21 to choose one "of these *men* which have companied with us" to take the place of Judas Iscariot. The Spirit led the church, according to the first part of Acts 6, to appoint seven men of good report to be the first to occupy the office of deacon. The Jerusalem council, recorded in Acts 15, was an all-male church council, and the decision of the council was to appoint "leading men" to go with Paul and Barnabas to Antioch to inform the church there of the church's decisions.

That the New Testament Scripture teaches that men shall occupy the special offices is plain from the passages which speak of the qualifications of officebearers, I Timothy 3 and Titus 1. These passages speak very clearly of men, not women, as elders and deacons in the church. Among the qualifications listed is that the officebearers must be the husband of one wife, and these passages expressly do not say the wife of one husband. There simply was no question in the mind of the apostle or in the mind of the early church as to God's will that men should be the ministers, elders, and deacons.

Besides this, there are especially two passages of the New Testament that expressly forbid women to occupy the offices. I Corinthians 14:34, 35 is the first of these passages: "Let your women keep silence in the churches: for it is not permitted unto them to speak; but they are commanded to be under obedience, as also saith the law. And if they will learn any thing, let them ask their husbands at home: for it is a shame for women to speak in the church."

Really, this passage is so utterly plain that its explanation ought to be obvious to anyone who is able to read the English language. The apostle calls the women to keep silence in the church. That does not mean that women may not talk inside a church building. That women are not allowed to speak means that they are not allowed to speak in the sense of preach or teach in God's church. The official ministering of the Word of God, which is, by the way, the work not simply of the minister but of all the officebearers, elders and deacons too, that is forbidden to women.

The second passage is I Timothy 2:11, 12: "Let the woman learn in silence with all subjection. But I suffer not a woman to teach, not to usurp authority over the man, but to be in silence." The apostle is speaking in this passage of the public worship services of the church. According to I Timothy 3:15, the first epistle to Timothy concerns proper behavior in the house of God, the church of God. Proper behavior for women in God's house, now, is that they NOT teach. For a woman to teach is improper behavior. Again — in the church. The women are not forbidden absolutely to teach. They may, and they must, teach their children at home. They may stand in the place of the parent in the Christian school and teach the covenant children. They must teach in the sense of speak and witness to all those with whom they come into contact day by day. They may teach Sunday School and teach one another in the Bible study societies of the church. In Titus 2:4, 5 Paul calls the older women to teach the younger women to be good wives and mothers. But they may not teach in the church. The woman is forbidden to occupy the pulpit and to preach.

More than this, Paul forbids them "to usurp authority over the man." The woman may not occupy the office of ruling elder. A woman who does this is a "usurper," that is, she acts on her own authority, not on the authority of God.

Rather, the woman is to learn in silence. She IS to learn; she is to grow in her knowledge and understanding of God's Word. But she is to do this in silence. That does not mean without talking. Literally, the apostle says "in quietness," that is, tending to her own affairs and in her own God-given place, not intruding into affairs which God has assigned to the men of the church.

She is to do this "with all subjection." Subjection is obedience. "All" subjection is total obedience.

The ground or reason for the apostle's teaching here is twofold. First of all, as in I Corinthians 11, the apostle appeals to creation: "For Adam was first formed, then Eve" (vs. 13). God created Adam first, and then He made Eve. And not only was Adam made by God before the woman, but the woman was made out of and for the man. In I

Corinthians 11:8, 9 the apostle says, "For the man is not of the woman; but the woman for the man."

And secondly, Adam was not deceived but the woman being deceived was found in the transgression (vs. 14). Now that does not mean that Adam did not sin and did not fall. We know better. Adam, however, was not deceived in the way in which the woman was deceived. The woman was deceived first, and the woman was utterly and thoroughly deceived. She took the lead in the fall; she was the one who talked to the serpent, was deceived by the serpent's temptation, and she became the occasion for Adam to fall. Her usurping to herself authority that had not been given to her played a crucial role in the original fall of the race. As a consequence: she shall not teach, nor usurp authority over the man, but be in silence.

An Examination of Certain Arguments for Ordination of Women

In spite of this clear teaching of the Scriptures which forbids women to occupy church office, the proponents of women in office put forward several arguments to overthrow this teaching of the Scriptures and to support their position that the church must open up the offices to women. We ought to examine the outstanding arguments of those who are seeking the ordination of women.

There is, first of all, the argument that appeals to certain women in the Old Testament who occupied the office of prophet. The Old Testament does speak of three prophetesses: Miriam, Moses' sister; Deborah, who was both a prophetess and a judge; and Hulda. Three things are worthy of note, however. First, these are the only recorded exceptions in the whole of the Old Testament to the obvious general rule that men were to occupy the offices. Secondly, in two of these cases, those of Deborah and Hulda, the spiritual condition of Israel was very low. They were raised up by God in times of great apostasy. The reason God raised them up and set them in the office of prophet was simply that there were no men in Israel fit to hold the office. And thirdly, it was by direct, special revelation that God called these women to office. They were prophets, that is, those to whom God gave direct, immediate revelation. We could accept women in office if this were still so today. But God does no longer give special revelations. The conclusion is obvious: there can be no women officebearers.

Secondly, the argument is put forward that the woman's general submission to the man, and specifically her submission in the church which takes the form of her not serving in the offices, is an aspect of the curse and is based solely on the consequences of sin and the fall. Appeal is made to Genesis 3:16, "Unto the woman he said, I will greatly multiply thy sorrow and thy conception; in sorrow thou shalt bring forth children; and thy desire shall be to thy husband, and he shall rule over thee." These were the words of curse that God pronounced against the woman on account of the fall. The next verses record God's curse over the man, that the ground would be cursed for his sake and that from now on he would have to work in the sweat of his face.

This argument runs something like this. As originally created by God, Adam and Eve stood in perfect equality. The fall into sin destroyed that equality, so that now the woman was placed in subjection to the man as part of God's judgment over her. Part of the work of Christ is to redeem the woman from this aspect of sin and the curse. In keeping with this work of Christ, the church ought to exert herself to elevate the position of the woman, restore her to her original equality, and make it possible for her to serve more completely and fully in the church. Just as we try to alleviate the effects of sin by anesthesia and pain-relievers for child-birth, and air-conditioned tractors for work, so we should attempt to alleviate the headship of man based solely on the fall and sin.

Notice, that this argument rests on two basic presuppositions. Number one, there was no headship of man over woman before the fall, in the perfect creation order. And number two, the rule of the man over the woman is part of the curse, something therefore inherently evil, a consequence of sin.

Two points must be made in response to this argument. First, we agree with the permissibility of attempting to relieve the effects of the fall into sin. There is nothing wrong with that in itself. But we do that, not by removing the realities themselves that are mentioned in Genesis 3: childbirth, work, and the submission of the woman to the man. Those realities themselves were not the curse pronounced over the man and woman by God. But we do that by alleviating that which corrupts these realities. In the case of the man's rule over the woman, the apostles do that in the New Testament by exhorting husbands to love and honor, nourish and cherish their wives, and not be bitter against them.

Secondly, our response to this argument is that the Scriptures themselves never call women to be subject to men in marriage or in the church because of the effects of sin and the fall. Consistently, the New Testament Scriptures appeal to the creation order, the pre-fall arrangement of things as establishing the principle of the woman's submission. The fact is that it is God's creation order, as evidenced in Genesis 1 and 2, that is the solid basis for the New Testament prohibition of women exercising authority in the offices of the church or in marriage and the home. That is I Corinthians 11:8, 9; I Timothy 2:13; and Ephesians 5.

A third argument for women in church office is the constant appeal to Galatians 3:28. In their use of this passage those advocating women in office remind us of a dog who has only one bark. The text reads: "There is neither Jew nor Greek, there is neither bond nor free, there is neither male nor female: for ye are all one in Christ Jesus." Let it be said, that this text has absolutely nothing to do with the question of women in church office. This is not the subject of the passage or of the context. And an appeal to this passage is entirely beside the point. The subject of Galatians 3:28 is salvation, and the enjoyment of salvation through the gift of faith in Jesus Christ. The point of the apostle is that salvation and faith are not confined to one limited sector of the human race. The New Testament church of Jesus Christ is a catholic, or universal church. Salvation is enjoyed not only by Jews, but also Greeks; not only by free men, but also slaves; not only by white men, but also black, red, and yellow men; not only by men (males), but also women (females). As far as the gift of salvation is concerned, it is the same as with the need for salvation: there is no difference between men and women.

Another argument for women in office, one of the most commonly heard arguments, is that not to ordain women into the offices wastes the gifts of women. If the church does not accede to the ordination of women, the church is guilty of squandering its resources and wasting women's gifts.

This argument is ridiculous, and amounts only to an emotional appeal for women in office. At issue is not the question whether or not women have gifts, or whether they ought to use their gifts, or whether the church ought to be diligent to employ the gifts of the women. But the issue concerns WHERE those gifts are to be employed. The same Holy Spirit who bestows gifts upon the members of the church is also the author of Scripture, also the Scriptures that forbid women to occupy office. Are we to suppose that the Holy Spirit would contradict Himself?

What About the Office of Deacon?

Although some agree that women may not be ordained to the office of minister or elder, they are willing to concede that there may be women deacons in the church. They argue, first, that a deacon would not have to teach or rule. And secondly, they appeal in support of their contention to two passages of Scripture which, to their mind, speak of women in the office of deacon: Romans 16:1 and I Timothy 5:9ff.

The view that women could easily be ordained as deacons because they would not have to teach or rule is mistaken. For the deacons, too, teach and have authority over the members of the church. Sharing in the office of Christ, they too, along with ministers and elders, share in Christ's authority. To occupy an office, in the nature of the case, is to occupy a position of authority. That is why a requirement for the deacons, as well as for the elders in I Timothy 3, is that they are "ruling their children and their own houses well." That requirement arises out of the fact that they must share in the rule of the church. And the fact of the matter is that in the course of their work the deacons must give some instruction and teaching officially and on behalf of the church of Jesus Christ. They do not simply write out checks and pay the bills.

The appeal to I Timothy 5:9ff. fails to prove the permissibility of women deacons. For, first, the apostle deliberately does not refer to the women mentioned here as "deacons" or "deaconesses," but simply as "women." Secondly, that which makes it impossible to appeal to this passage in support of the ordination of women into the office of deacon is that the apostle requires that these women be widows and that they be widows of at least sixty years of age. Those who appeal to this passage want the office opened up to ALL women.

Nor does the appeal to Romans 16:1, the example of Phebe, prove the permissibility of women deacons. The passage reads in the King James Version as follows: "I commend unto you Phebe our sister, which is a servant of the church which is at Cenchrea." The argument from this passage rests on the fact that the word translated "servant" may also be translated "deacon" or "deaconess." This is the translation offered by both the Revised Standard Version and Phillips.

There is no question about it that "deaconess" is a proper translation of the word "servant" that is used here. The question, however, is whether it is a proper translation in this particular passage. Or are the translators of the King James Version correct when they translate "servant"?

It should be noted that this word "servant" occurs in the New Testament in many different connections. It refers to servants, both male and female, in households; to servants of kings; to servants who are called to be obedient to their masters; to servants of God who occupy positions of government in the state. Besides, the word occurs in a host of passages where it MUST be translated "servant" and where it would be impossible and make no sense to translate it by "deacon" or "deaconess." You can check this yourself by referring to a good concordance. The point is that one cannot conclude simply on the basis of the term itself, that Phebe was a deacon in the church. And in the light of the rest of the New Testament, she could not have been. She was a godly woman who served her fellow believers in the church at Cenchrea, and who was highly commended by the apostle, but she was NOT an officebearer.

The Underlying Issue in the Debate Over Women in Church Office

That brings us to the final argument of those who are advocating women in church office. At the same time, with this argument the underlying issue in connection with the debate over women in office is brought clearly to the foreground.

What is that underlying issue? The Bible in plain language forbids women to teach or rule in the church. One simply cannot find support for women officebearers in the Scriptures. What do they do then who advocate women in office? They deny that these Scriptures apply in our time and to our culture. Surely, Paul in I Corinthians 14 and I Timothy 2 was forbidding women to hold office. But the apostle's teaching there is to be understood in the light of his Jewish training, and in the light of early New Testament culture. We must understand, we are told, that the Scriptures are time-bound and culturally conditioned. What the apostle wrote applied to his times and his culture, but it does not apply anymore in our times and in our culture. The underlying issue, therefore, is Scripture and the church's confession of the inspiration, infallibility, and authority of Holy Scripture.

Others see this as the issue, too. In a fine article in *Christianity Today* magazine (April 9, 1976) on the question of women in office, George W. Knight III states:

> But I am distressed that some who have written on the subject (women in office, RC) seem to be abandoning the inerrancy of Scripture and the authority of its teaching. Even some who claim to be evangelical Christians, to submit to the authority of God and his Word, seem willing to appeal to the passages in Scripture that support their position and to minimize other passages or declare them to be either wrong or only culturally relative and not normative, even when these passages themselves claim to be normative and not culturally relative.

This is exactly what Paul K. Jewett does in his book *The Ordination of Women* (William B. Eerdmans Publishing Company, Grand Rapids, MI, 1980). Jewett is professor of systematic theology at Fuller Theological Seminary in California. In his book Jewett is bold to assert that Paul's teaching is simply a reflection of an erroneous rabbinical view. He is bold to assert that Paul's understanding of Genesis 1 and 2 is wrong. He is bold to assert that Paul's teaching is simply conditioned by the culture in which he lived and need not be followed anymore today.

In a editorial in *The Banner,* editor Andrew Kuyvenhoven came down for basically this same position.

> There is no doubt in my mind that Paul was prescribing a restricted role to women in the service of worship when he wrote I Cor. 14:34 and I Tim. 2:12. However, the reasons for the restrictions were local, cultural, and therefore temporal. Paul could appeal to what was in his day a common moral judgment: a woman speaking in church looked "bad," "shameful" (I Cor. 14:35). But when such an appeal can no longer be made, the special apostolic prescription is also removed (*The Banner,* January 23, 1984).

Our response to this argument is simple: We deny it! It is false and wrong, and is a fatal concession of the doctrine of Holy Scripture. If this argument is allowed to stand in the church, the church has lost everything. The issue is not women in office. That is just an aside, a little aside. The issue is the infallibility and consequent authority of Holy

Scripture. The position for women in office is only one more attack, among so many others today, against Holy Scripture itself. In the end, if the position that the Scriptures are culturally conditioned and time-bound is allowed to stand, it will be possible to set aside every doctrine and every commandment of the Scriptures.

This assertion that the apostle's teaching is conditioned by the culture and times in which he lived stands directly over against the apostle's own assertion that what he taught is the will of God, an assertion which the apostle makes in the very passages in which he prohibits the women to occupy the offices of the church. In I Timothy 2 the apostle asserts that the prohibition of women in office is based on God's will expressed already in the creation order. Already in verse 7 of the chapter he had expressly said concerning the instruction that he was about to give, "I speak the truth in Christ, and lie not." In I Corinthians 14:34 the apostle states that his instruction has its foundation in the law, in the will of God revealed already in the Old Testament law: "Let your women keep silence in the churches: for it is not permitted unto them to speak; but they are commanded to be under obedience, as also saith the law." The apostle insists on exactly the opposite of what men are saying today, that his teaching was grounded in the abiding will of God revealed in the law.

I ask you, do you suppose for one minute that the Lord Jesus would allow Himself to be pressured by the cultural situation of His day? Did He ever cave in to the prejudices and wrongs of the culture of His day? Are we really to suppose that the One who forgave adulterers, ate with publicans and sinners, who was not afraid to point out the errors and hypocrisy of the religious leaders of His day, was actually afraid of offending the culture of His day? Was this the reason why He didn't appoint any women disciples? To ask these questions is to answer them.

One wonders! One really wonders about this cultural question! Who really are the products of their culture: Jesus? The apostles? Or those today who are pushing for the ordination of women? The question arises whether or not, after all, it is not the modern advocates of women in office who have not caved in to a godless, antichristian culture out of which the whole modern women's movement has arisen? One wonders!

In any case, let us be clear, if the modern view wins the day, number one, the entire doctrine of Scripture's infallibility and authority goes out the window. And number two, the perspicuity or clarity of the Scriptures is overthrown and no ordinary Christian will be able to read and to understand the Bible anymore. He will have to trust the experts, who know all the cultural, linguistic, philosophical, and historical considerations which influenced the writers of the Bible. As happened in the Romish Church prior to the Reformation, the Bible will be taken out of the hands of the ordinary people and once again confined to a hierarchy of "experts." God spare us this calamity!

Our Calling to Stand Against This Movement

The church today and the individual believer must stand over against the movement to ordain women into church office. Whatever the cost, whatever sacrifice is required, whatever personal injury is suffered, we must stand! We must maintain the Scriptural position, without compromise. Martin Luther once said to those who were hedging in his day:

> If I profess with the loudest voice and clearest exposition every portion of the truth of God, except precisely that little point which the world and the devil are at that moment attacking, I am not confessing Christ. Where the battle rages, there the loyalty of the soldier is proved, and to be steady on all the battle front besides is mere flight and disgrace if he flinches at that point.

This stand of the church and of the believer must be a thorough-going and consistent stand. It must be a position that forbids the women to occupy the offices of minister, elder, and deacon. Besides that, the women are forbidden to teach catechism classes. The Reformed position is that catechism instruction is as much official teaching in the church as is the preaching of the Word on the Lord's day. Nor ought women to be given the right to vote at the congregational meetings of the church. The congregational meeting is an official gathering of the church. For a woman to vote at a congregational meeting is for a woman to exercise some authority, to enter into the government of the church. That is prohibited. There is an old proverb out of the Far East that the time to keep the camel out of your tent is when the camel sticks his nose into your tent. You let his nose in and you may be sure that his body will soon be following along. Reformed churches do well to keep the nose of this camel out of their tent.

The Positive Calling of the Women

This stand of the church prohibiting women to occupy the offices must also be a stand that carefully lays before the women their positive calling in the church. That positive calling is summarized in I Timothy 2:15, "Notwithstanding she shall be saved in child-bearing, if they continue in faith and charity and holiness with sobriety." The hue and cry of the modern woman's movement has its source in the neglect and despising by the women of the positive calling which God gives them.

The Scriptures call women to their proper task of child-bearing. That is the unique and glorious calling that God has given to women in the church. Carrying out this calling they find their fulfillment. God gives women all kinds of opportunity to teach and to rule — their children in the fear of His name. With a view to His calling God has blessed the women with many gifts, physically, emotionally, and spiritually, gifts which God has not given to the men. In the way of their carrying out of this calling, God's church is born into the world and gathered. In this way Christ came into the world, born of a woman the Bible says, and God did not need and God did not use a man.

How this calling of the women needs to be emphasized today! How women today refuse to carry out their God-given calling, by means of birth-control, or still worse, by means of the cold-blooded murder of abortion. What a terrible judgment of God rests upon them!

The apostle goes so far as to say in I Timothy 2:15, "she shall be *saved* in child-bearing." Oh, to be sure, the women, just like the men, are saved by the blood of Jesus Christ. But they are saved in the way of childbearing. They are not saved in the way of preaching, not in the way of ruling, and not in the way of administering the mercies of Christ in the church. They are saved in the way of child-bearing.

What about those women who are past the time of child-bearing, or to whom the Lord does not grant the privilege of bearing children? Have they no place in the church? They certainly do! Let them be known as was Dorcas for her good works and for her almsdeeds. Let them visit the fatherless, the widows, the sick, and the aged in their affliction. Let them stand in the place of the parents in the Christian school. Let them assist the poor and be involved in all of the ways they can be involved in helping God's church. But let them not be ministers or elders or deacons.

This is the teaching of the Word of God. What do you say? Say with me, "Choose you this day whom ye will serve; but as for me and my house, we will serve the Lord" (Joshua 24:15).

Women Serving God

or
The Proper Place of the Deaconess in the Church

Steven R. Key

Although the Scriptures are clear on the subject of women officebearers in the church, an aspect of the Scriptures which is often forgotten is the fact that the Scriptures do give work in the church to women. Rev. Steven Key deals with this subject in an important chapter as he points out how much the Scriptures really have to say about women's place in the church as well as in the home.

Women Serving God

Probably never before has the role of women in the church been so much on the foreground of controversy and debate as it is in our generation. A controversy that began already in the early part of this century, concerning whether or not a woman may vote in congregational meetings of Reformed churches, has developed through the years into a controversy over whether she may serve in the special offices of the church — whether that be minister, elder, or deacon.

It is not my intention, however, to enter at length into that controversy. We face the question rather: how can we promote the work of women in the church? According to the Scriptures, women are indeed called to serve as deaconesses in the church of our Lord Jesus Christ and to use their gifts in the service of God, His church and His people. This calling we must understand properly.

There is no question but that we deal here with a highly emotional issue in much of the church world today. In those churches which historically are closest to us, and in which many of us have our roots, we have observed a war taking place for several years now. The two sides in that war both insist that they are defending the place of women in the church. One side in particular claims to be promoting the work of deaconesses (as well as women elders and pastors). All the participants in that battle would like to call it a *holy* war. But on one side of that battle in particular there has been such a departure from the Holy Word of God, that it has come to be seen by us as a very *unholy* war. In fact, there are those who openly attack the Bible in their self-proclaimed "promotion" of women in the church. In a paper recently published by "The Committee for Women in the Christian Reformed Church," the author referred to the Bible as "hopelessly patriarchal because of its emphasis on men," and termed the Bible a hindrance to women (reprinted in the ***Christian Renewal,*** Sept. 3, 1990, pp. 10, 11). I do not think the devil himself would dare be so bold in his opposition to God's Word.

It is my desire with the church of old to promote the place of women in the church, to promote the calling of women to serve as deaconesses in the church. I intend to do so on the basis of the Word of God. I do so unequivocably and without apology. But that also means that the

Scriptures are going to determine what is meant by the term "deaconess," and the Scriptures are going to determine the calling encompassed in that idea of women serving as deaconesses in Christ's church and in our own Protestant Reformed churches.

In the first place, it is necessary to consider briefly what is meant by serving God as a deaconess — and what is *not* meant. Secondly, I want to give some historical perspectives of this calling. And finally, I want to conclude with some examination of Scriptural examples, leaving us with God's record of women who have served Him faithfully and who now are partaking of their heavenly reward.

What is Meant by Serving God as a Deaconess

When we insist that there is a calling for women to serve as deaconesses in the church, we are *not* saying that that calling for a woman is the same as the calling given to those men called to the office of deacon.

The word "deacon" is translated in different ways in the Bible. It is most often translated simply as "servant" — and correctly so, for its general meaning is taken from a verb which means "to minister to the needs of others." Outside the context of the particular office God has instituted in His church, everyone is called to be a deacon or a deaconess. That is, as we read in Matthew 23:11, "But he that is greatest among you shall be your servant." And that word "servant" is *diakonos*, the same word translated deacon in I Timothy 3. Obviously there is a difference in connotation in the way Jesus uses the word in Matthew 23:11 and the way Paul uses it in I TImothy 3.

To be a servant in the church is something distinct from serving God in that office of deacon which He instituted through His apostles. That particular office was instituted as a representation of Christ's priestly office, administering His mercy to those in need and at the same time freeing ministers and elders to serve more diligently in their peculiar callings. The qualifications for a deacon are clearly set forth in I Timothy 3. And those qualifications exclude women from the office. The office of deacon instituted by Christ is also an office that has only one essential calling, and that is to bring the Word of God.

Each office in the church of Jesus Christ, whether that of minister or that of elder or that of deacon, is an office of the ministry of the Word.

Those who cannot bring the Word of God in accordance with the calling of the offices, cannot be officebearers in the church. Each one functioning in an office must bring the Word of God according to the unique character of his office, whether that be in the office of the ministry, the office of the Christian governing of the church, or the office of administering the mercies of Christ. And because the offices all are offices in which the Word of God is administered, women are excluded from functioning in those offices. That is not because women occupy an inferior position in the church. That is not because they lack *gifts*.

How often have not we heard the argument that to keep women out of the special offices of the church is to stifle their gifts. That has nothing to do with the question. I will grant you that there are women who have more knowledge and more gifts than men who serve in those offices. I am willing to grant you that proposition. But again, the argument concerning the suppression of women's spiritual gifts does not apply with respect to the question whether or not they may occupy the office of the deacon in the church of Jesus Christ. The reason is very simple, if you receive the instruction of the Scriptures. God has given women a different role in which to use those very gifts He has given them.

God has given women a different role from the men, a very blessed role, as becomes clear in the light of the Bible. Women have an all-important and blessed role in the church, but a role in which, according to I Corinthians 14:34ff. and elsewhere, they are to "keep silent in the churches: for (God says) it is not permitted unto them to speak; but they are commanded to be under obedience, as also saith the law. And if they will learn anything, let them ask their husbands at home: for it is a shame for women to speak in the church." The inspired apostle Paul enjoins the church in I Timothy 2:9ff. that women adorn themselves with *good works*. But those good works are completely separate from the good works performed in the special offices of the church. For Paul also writes, "Let the women learn in silence with all subjection. But I suffer not a women to teach, nor to usurp authority over the man, but to be in silence." And the reason for that silence is in no way centered in the culture of Paul's day. But it is rooted in the very creation ordinance of God. "For Adam was first formed, then Eve."

It appears that the past two or three generations are the first in the history of the church that are embarrassed by human beings coming in two genders! The reason, of course, is that the unbiblical thinking of modern humanity is desirable to our sinful flesh. Man does not *want* God's way! But it ought not surprise us who are in the church and who believe God created man and formed the women out of the man to be an help meet for him — it ought not surprise us that God would want to keep that distinction which He created *good*. When He created man and woman in the way that He did, giving them different roles and calling them each to a distinct service, He beheld that work of His hands and said, "It is very good." God is not pleased when women and men apologize for that distinction, when they try to break it down, when they attempt to confuse the distinct callings of men and women.

Historical Perspective

With that being said, however, it is not my intention to continue with a lengthy criticism of how the broader church world has corrupted the place of women and the institution of the offices in the church. There has been much written about that error. The danger for us who hold to the biblical teaching of the special offices of the church is that we approach the problem of the role of women far too negatively. We must be careful that, in our scripturally-based denial of the office of deacon to women, we do not at the same time suppress their God-given gifts. It is unfortunate that not much has been written about that positive calling of women as deaconesses. Certainly the Bible's teaching is not exhausted when we say that women may not preach and may not exercise any of the special offices in the church. There is much they may do, have been doing through the years, and should be encouraged to do.

In the first place, let it be said that there are specific callings peculiar to women, callings set forth in different places throughout the Scriptures. I would urge all women in the church to study Proverbs 31, e.g., as well as the writings of Paul to Timothy and Titus, and I Peter 3, to mention just a handful of those passages applicable to women and particularly to wives. The calling set forth in those passages is basic to any other labors of service you may perform in the church. That is to say, if a woman lives in rebellion against God and His Word in those passages, she is unworthy and incapable of serving Him to His glory in any other aspect of the church. But without developing the teachings of those passages, I would have you focus your attention more narrowly on another calling for the women who belong to Jesus and are His followers. To be a deaconess is the calling of women in the church. And to be a deaconess is to be a servant of God in the very role He has given you.

That calling has found emphasis in the church throughout history, from the time Jesus' apostles walked on this earth.

We ought to be reminded, in the first place, that Jesus Christ, by His death and resurrection, elevated the status of women to the highest spiritual level possible. It is a sad commentary of our total depravity and the effects of man's fall into sin that women have been subject to various degrees of inferiority and degradation from the time that Eve forsook her role as a helper fit for Adam, her head. Throughout the history of the world her position has ranged from one of enslavement and abuse to that of mere tolerance — and that ofttimes even within the realm of the church.

Scripture and historical records make clear that the place of women in the church and the attitude of women and of men towards women needed much correction by God's prophets and apostles. We find that instruction and correction already in the Old Testament. In Proverbs 31, for example, the woman, that is, a *godly* woman, is certainly elevated to a high place of honor. And God held before His people and holds before women in particular many examples of godliness among women in the Old Testament, women who personified the woman described in Proverbs 31. We are pointed to such women as Sarah, Leah, Ruth, and Hannah — in each case an example to covenant girls and women of the truth that the lofty position in God's covenant and kingdom for women is found in obedience to their heads, and in faithfulness to their calling as wives and mothers. And I thank God for such women in the church today.

But especially when Christ came and ministered, and when He continued His ministry through His apostles, new light was shed on the beautiful place of women in the church. Although not affecting their roles as such, Christianity places male and female on an equal spiritual footing in Christ. Galatians 3:28: "There is neither male nor female: for ye are all one in Christ Jesus." That is to say, men and women who belong to Jesus Christ are *together* prophets, priests, and kings in the office of believer. Yet, we are prophets, priests, and kings within those very roles given us by God in creation. Being partakers of the Spirit of Christ affects the outlook and zeal with which a godly woman exercises her calling before the face of God.

It is striking how often women are mentioned in the New Testament, and how prominent was the role they played as women in the early church. Women surrounded Jesus during His earthly sojourn, serving Him and listening to His teaching. Women were the first to hear the resurrection gospel. And after Jesus' death and resurrection and His ascension into heaven, women continued to have a very prominent place in the development and expansion of the early church. In many of the places the apostle Paul visited and preached on his missionary journeys, his audiences were apparently made up predominantly, if not exclusively, of women. I think that is indication of how important women are to the church in the particular place and calling God has given them.

That elevated status and lofty calling has continued throughout the history of the church, in spite of those who have attempted to corrupt that calling by criticizing and tearing apart the God-ordained place of women in the church and bringing confusion to that place of women in the church.

The prominent role which women have played in the history of the church is seen, first of all, in the fruits of motherhood. When Christ elevated the marriage bond by explicitly setting it forth as a picture of the mystical union of Christ with His church, He thereby also elevated the calling of the wife and mother. Motherhood is the God-appointed career and calling of most covenant women. And if the young women especially, also through the instruction of the older women according to Titus 2, look at their calling from the viewpoint of the Scriptures and see the glory of motherhood as the Scriptures set it forth, they will count themselves extraordinarily blessed to be able to hold such a lofty place in God's kingdom.

Through all the history of the church, up until these past apostatizing generations in the last days, the church has extolled women as God-fearing wives and mothers. Timothy is one example of the influence godly women can have in God's church by exercising their calling as mothers and grandmothers. That influence reached far beyond Timothy! Many of the church fathers attributed their faith to the influence of godly mothers. When you read the writings of church history, the personal writings of the church fathers, you find numerous references to godly women. Probably the most well-known is the mother of Augustine, Monica, to whom he pays loving tribute in his *Confessions* and *Letters*. It is within the marriage state and as mothers that most women exercise their initial service of God in the church.

But when we think about the idea of deaconesses and women serving God, we probably focus a little more narrowly on particular callings the women may have in the church apart from that high calling of wife and mother. There are in the church, after all, those who in the providence of God are not married, as well as those whose married state has been cut short by the death of their husbands. The church has also recognized throughout history the important place such women have within the broader fellowship of believers. In fact, among the widows of the church, there was apparently at one time a society to which some widows belonged and which society had as its constitution the calling to serve as proper deaconesses in the church. Although we are not given much information concerning this society of widows, there is reference to such in I Timothy 5:9ff. So strictly did those widows devote their lives and labors to serving God in His church, that there were stringent entrance requirements placed upon those who would serve in that society of deaconesses. They had to be at least 60 years old. The demands of their service required that they must be able to devote their time to their calling, not being interrupted in their service by the care of their own small children or by the desire to remarry. Moreover, a woman who entered that number had to have shown in her life that she was qualified for that service. She had to be a woman well spoken of, a woman of whom others could testify that she was devoted to godly works. She must have brought up children, a woman who understood the importance of her role in the covenant. She had to be one who understood that women shall be saved in childbearing. She had to understand her God-given position toward her husband and toward the kingdom of God. If she was to serve in this society, she had to have shown a history of hospitality, a *giving* attitude. She must not have been a woman too self-centered to have her own schedule interrupted by a stranger, but one who had shown an interest in entertaining visitors. For the work of a deaconess calls for qualities where one is interested not in self, but in others. Furthermore, Paul writes that the candidate for this society of widow deaconesses must be one who has washed the feet of saints. There is a picture of humility, of giving for those for whom Christ died. One who will wash the feet of saints, one of the lowliest jobs in the communion of saints, is certainly willing to do any other lowly task on behalf of the saint in need. Moreover, when affliction becomes the lot of God's people, she should not be found negligent but willing to provide that nursing and hospice care, if you will. In summary, "if she have diligently followed every good work," she may be admitted to this society of widows serving God.

Those are some of the things we learn from the New Testament and from church history concerning the important place of women serving God. There indeed is a place — a very important place — for deaconesses in the church, women who devote their lives to serving God and the saints, apart from the special offices which belong only to the men of God's choosing.

Scriptural Examples

Having painted an overview of some of the historical perspectives of deaconesses in the church, allow me to point out a couple more passages from the Scriptures which shed some important light on this subject of women serving God.

Women who want to serve God, women who would be deaconesses, ministering servants in the church of Jesus Christ, are not limited to any particular office or society within the church. There have been many saints, godly women, whose lives of service to the church are recorded for our example.

I call your attention to Acts 9:36.

In Acts 9:36ff., we read of a certain woman disciple in Joppa. Her Hebrew name was Tabitha, her Greek name Dorcas. We are told in Acts 9:36 that Dorcas was "full of good works and almsdeeds which she did." Good works denote works of piety in general, a very broad category. And that Dorcas was *full* of good works indicates that her good works were multiple and varied. "Almsdeeds" are specific good works, i.e., works of mercy. To do alms is to give of money, time, and strength to those in need. That is the work of a deaconess. Not only that, but it is to give of one's belongings and time and strength to the glory of God, thus showing the mercy of God in Jesus Christ.

Going on to verse 39, we notice that Dorcas was apparently a seamstress, and a gifted one at that. But instead of enriching herself financially by sewing only for money, she enriched her soul by sewing out of the love of God and His church. She used her gift for the welfare of God's people. And it becomes evident in these verses that she devoted much of her good works and almsdeeds to the widows of the church. It is possible, given her interest in widows, that she herself was a widow. But she certainly saw a need in the church concerning those women who had been widowed. And she responded to that need.

We ought to remember that in that time when there were no life insurance policies and pension plans and social security systems and the like such as we have today, the widows were usually very poor. That was the case also because in many places families were not taking care of their own, as we gather from Paul's admonition in I Timothy 5:16. Another factor was the failure of the church to live up to her calling in caring for the widows and those in need. That great failure, that had permeated the Jewish religious institute, had also carried over into the church as we learn from James 1:27. Dorcas, however, labored to provide for many widows by making and giving to them clothing.

Now, I submit to you that although the times in which we live are different and not many widows in the church are destitute and in need of clothing, many of the elderly women are in need of the care of women in particular. Some may be widowed. They know the pain of loneliness, and the need for visits and companionship. There are many elderly women in retirement or nursing homes. In one degree or another, most bear the afflictions of a frail human body. And their starvation is not for food, but for the visits of God's people, and particularly women. And although it is true that nobody really understands the need until having experienced it, we all must learn from the testimony of the Scriptures and God's people that women are needed for the care of the widows in the church, just as was Dorcas.

I call your attention also to the last chapter of Paul's epistle to the Romans, and particularly to the greetings found in the first 16 verses of that chapter.

Immediately you find reference to Phebe, a servant, deaconess, in the church at Cenchrea. Verses 1 and 2 belong not to the Christian greetings extended in the chapter, but rather might be considered a certificate of recommendation on behalf of the sister in the faith named Phebe.

A couple of things we should notice in the first two verses of Romans 16. In the first place, when Paul speaks of Phebe as our "sister" he is using a common expression which is also significant. When the Scriptures and when we speak of the people of God as brothers and sisters in the Lord, then we are referring to the truth that the church of Christ constitutes a family. We are brothers and sisters in the one household of faith. That means that our calling of service in the church extends far beyond that calling within our immediate blood families. We must nurture one another in the faith and provide for *all* our brothers and sisters whom we see in need. In the second place, Phebe was not an officebearer. But she did occupy a prominent place in the church. In an unofficial way, but in a blessed and energetic way, Phebe had been laboring in the Lord, helping many, and especially Paul. She cared for the saints according to their needs, took them into her home and ministered unto them. That is how she fulfilled her calling as a deaconess in Christ's church. Evidently Phebe was the one who would deliver this letter to the church at Rome, which is why the apostle commends her to them and urges them to receive her as becometh saints.

In verses 3 through 5 of Romans 16, we find greetings of Paul to Priscilla and Aquila, his helpers in Christ Jesus. Priscilla, of course, was a woman. She and her husband risked their necks for Paul. They showed themselves willing to lay down their lives for the brother. According to I John 3:16, "Hereby perceive we the love of God." No greater love could be shown by a deaconess. Furthermore, Paul calls them "my helpers in Christ Jesus." Paul was not ashamed to call those two, one of whom was a woman, his helpers in the gospel.

There is an important point here that I want to apply to the calling of women in particular. We ministers of the gospel need the full service of women in the church. To fill an office in the church of Jesus Christ belongs only to those men whom God has appointed; but to labor for the cause of the gospel, either publicly or privately, belongs to every

Christian according to the gifts bestowed upon him or her by God Himself, as is clear in Romans 12. Faithful labors of the ministry and the offices of elder and deacon are great, far more demanding than what most realize. The needs of the church are innumerable. And that means that the labors are far greater than one man or even a group of men. If women fail to exercise their calling of deaconesses in the church, the church suffers. And it suffers greatly. That certainly is emphasized by implication in Romans 16.

When we proceed into the rest of the chapter, we find a striking phenomenon in that inspired record. Many of those whom the apostle mentions are *women*. Besides Priscilla, special greetings are given to Mary, Tryphena, and Tryphosa, the beloved Persis, as well as others, nine in all. Those women are said to labor in the Lord. Let it never be said of godly women that they do not occupy a place of importance in the church of Jesus Christ. The women named by the apostle did not labor in an office in the church. They were not elders and deacons. Rather they held a different place just as important. They performed all kinds of work, as we can derive from other portions of the Scriptures. They visited the sick, they ministered to the needs of the saints, they gave instruction to the younger women "to be sober, to love their husbands, to love their children, to be discreet, chaste, keepers at home, good, obedient to their own husbands, that the word of God be not blasphemed" (Titus 2). They sewed, they cared for the elderly, they hosted strangers, even receiving angels unawares. A God-fearing woman does not have to be an elder or a deacon or a president of a society or even a Sunday school teacher to labor in the Lord. Christ says if you give a drink of water to a disciple, you labor in the Lord. And you will receive special mention.

The church is blessed that has godly women serving as deaconesses — not in the special offices, but as God has called them, to seek the welfare of the many members of His church.

It is not necessary, nor desirable, for a woman merely to fill her time or to seek more earthly goods by getting a job after the children are out of the house. There are many jobs available within the church and the broader circle of the church's diaconal obligations. Let me mention just a couple specific examples.

According to our Church Order, we have a calling to support

institutions of mercy—hospitals and nursing homes. Just about all the hospitals in the area have need of volunteers to assist in different areas. The same holds true with many of the nursing and rest homes. How many are there from your congregation who are shut-ins or who are in rest homes? Women might well ask themselves: When have I last visited them or done anything in caring for them? We read in James 1:27: "Pure religion and undefiled before God and the Father is this, To visit the fatherless and widows in their affliction, and to keep himself unspotted from the world."

I would also contend that women can have a meaningful ministry and can participate in a profitable way in their diaconal calling by counseling others in the church of Jesus Christ. Today counseling is usually seen as a highly specialized function, the exclusive province of those with at least a college master's degree in psychology and those with psychiatric training. We ought in no way belittle those who serve the church in those capacities. There are many times when professionals are needful in those fields. But do not forget, the Scriptures see counseling as a responsibility of the entire Christian fellowship. Women, as well as men, are covered by Paul's charge to the believers in Thessalonica: "Warn them that are unruly, comfort the feebleminded, support the weak, be patient toward all." When a woman of the church is unruly, a busy-body, spending her time sowing seeds of discord with her gossip, there is no one in a better position to warn her than another woman. A woman who is in weakened condition because of a physical or psychological affliction is often most comforted and supported by another woman who may have experienced the same affliction at another time. There are many problems that would never get to the minister, let alone to the psychiatrist, if they were faced up to by Christian women in the interactions of ordinary Christian fellowship and true friendship.

The Scriptures make clear that women also are to be teachers. That is certainly true of young women with families. It hardly needs to be said that they are to be teachers in the home, guiding their children in the precepts of Jehovah, showing them also how to live godly in marriage and as parents. But the Scriptures speak specifically of the calling of the "aged women," as Paul refers to them in Titus 2:3. Let me just define that phrase "aged women" as referring to women who are of a mature age. Their calling is "that they be in behavior as becometh holiness, not false accusers, not given to much wine, *teachers of good things;* that they may teach the young women to be sober, to love their husbands, to love their children, to be discreet, chaste, keepers at home, good, obedient to their own husbands, that the word of God be not blasphemed." That is their God-given calling. That is how they fulfill that which God gives them to do as deaconesses, ministering servants in His kingdom.

It was the sight of women so serving God that caused a Greek historian, and a heathen at that, to exclaim, "What women the Christians have!" In this day when the church can hardly be distinguished from the world, what would a historian write of us?

Let us remember, with respect to these various passages we have skimmed over in this chapter, the Holy Spirit mentions these women. And the church that receives the instruction of the Spirit recognizes that women have an important place in the labors of Christ — apart from the special offices of the church. Indeed, the acknowledgment of the apostle in Romans 16 for the women who labor in the Lord shows that the life of the church, her very vitality and spiritual welfare is dependent upon the presence of godly, virtuous women.

God gives virtuous women a place of excellency in His church. And the church is to receive her God-fearing women in the Lord. How often do we honor the wives and the women of the church, as the apostle holds them in esteem? How often do we pray for them and instruct them and guide them in their labors? May we as a church receive them from God with thanksgiving and encourage them in their faithful labors in the Lord. And may others say of our women and of us all, they have been with Jesus!